DODGE
VIPER

DANIEL F. CARNEY

MBI Publishing Company

First published in 2001 by MBI Publishing Company, Galtier Plaza, Suite 200, 380 Jackson Street, St. Paul, MN 55101-3885 USA

MBI Publishing Company books are also available at discounts in bulk quantity for industrial or sales-promotional use. For details write to Special Sales Manager at Motorbooks International Wholesalers & Distributors, Galtier Plaza, Suite 200, 380 Jackson Street, St. Paul, MN 55101-3885 USA.

Library of Congress Cataloging-in-Publication Data available
ISBN 0-7603-0984-1

Edited by Sam Moses
Designed by Katie Sonmor

Printed in Hong Kong

On the front cover: 1993 GTS Coupe. *John Lamm*

On the frontis: A new age and a new icon. The original, slightly grinning Viper icon has been replaced for the new generation car with this more serious, menacing image.

On the title page: 1996 RT/10 Roadster. *John Lamm*

On the last page: 1993 GTS Coupe. *John Lamm*

On the back cover: 2000 GTS/R race car concept. *John Lamm*

CONTENTS

The Viper is still the ultimate American performance icon. Here we are, 10 years after its introduction, and there's still nothing like it produced in the United States—or anywhere in the world—at anywhere near the price. It still attracts attention when you show up with it. It still turns heads.

Ten years later and it's still victorious in racing. Here is this 10-year-old design with a pushrod engine, and it's still cleaning the clocks of much more modern cars made by some of the great European companies.

Two-, three-, and four-year-old Vipers are holding their values extremely well. The Viper is still a sought-after automobile. After all this time, with no major aesthetic changes to the car in almost 10 years, that's almost unheard of.

I thought we wouldn't have any trouble building 2,000 a year, but I never suspected it would generate as much emotional energy as it did. What I didn't foresee, and didn't appreciate until we were well into making the car and had sold quite a few, was the degree of commitment, enthusiasm, and almost religious fervor and fanaticism for the Viper among its owners.

I've never met a lukewarm Viper owner. I've never met a guy who said, "Yeah, I've got one, but it's okay. I drive it occasionally. I thought I'd like to have one, but it's okay." I've never met anybody like that. They either have one (or more), love it, and are passionate about it, or they don't have one. In terms of owner satisfaction, owner loyalty, and degree of commitment to the car, it is unparalleled in the annals of the American industry.

What did the Viper do? Why am I proud today to have been associated with it? It is the first really credible American limited-production ultimate supercar that received perhaps even more respect in Europe than it received in the United States. People are going to say, "No, no, you are wrong. The Chevrolet Corvette is." The Chevy Corvette almost made it, but not quite.

I sure hoped they would still be building Vipers after 10 years, but I never thought it would take General Motors this long to react to it. I thought we would have a run of maybe five years, and then there would either be a 10-cylinder, 500-horsepower special-edition Mustang, or Chevrolet would do a 10-cylinder or 12-cylinder super Corvette. I thought that one of our American competitors would come out with a car to trump it. The astonishing thing to me is that after 10 years, nobody has.

—*Bob Lutz*

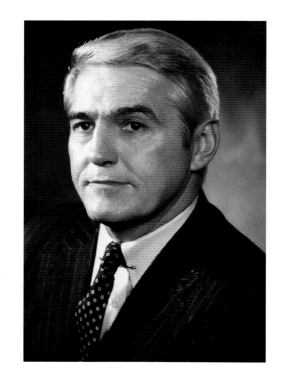

ACKNOWLEDGMENTS

The vast amount of information, knowledge, legend, and maybe a few tall tales relating to the history and development of the Dodge Viper made writing a book on the car an extremely daunting task. It seemed, at times, that a book whose goal was to provide a comprehensive history on the car was doomed to failure, because with every interview, more stories poured out. Finally, it became obvious that truly comprehensive coverage of the Viper would require commentary from hundreds, maybe thousands, of people, if not everyone who has ever laid eyes on the car. To see the Viper is to be affected by it.

Everyone, it seems, has a Viper story, even if it's simply recalling the first time they saw one in traffic. The people who helped design and build the car, obviously, have more directly related stories to tell, but there are so many of those people that it's impossible to include all the stories. The world may never know how many times Viper test mules caught fire, or at least puffed enough smoke to concern onlookers.

So I thank the many people who contributed their time and memories with me to make this book what it is. That obviously starts with the Viper's "four-fathers," who are responsible for bringing the car forth unto the world.

Bob Lutz was extremely patient in granting interviews in which he outlined the Viper's genesis and opined on the direction the car has taken since he relinquished control. Francois Castaing was gracious enough to squeeze our discussions into his globe-trotting schedule, and Tom Gale found time to provide his perspective on the Viper during the busy period preceding his retirement from the company. Carroll Shelby revealed in his typically candid manner that he had less to do with the Viper's design and development than is commonly believed, but he is credited with convincing then-chairman Lee Iacocca to approve the project in the first place. So without his effort, there would not likely have been a Viper.

Unofficial four-father Roy Sjoberg illuminated the hard work required to actually build the car imagined by the others, and he promises his own book on the nitty-gritty Viper gestation in the future. His recollections really put flesh on the bones of the story, because he knows not just what happened, but why and how.

The baton has passed to John Fernandez, who also provided excellent insight into the Viper's ongoing development and the all-new 2003 Viper. His comments, along with those of John Herlitz, Jim Julow, Herb Helbig, and Bob Champine, illustrate the continuing effort to maintain the Viper's status as king of the hill in all-out performance. Ken Payne gave us a unique inside view of how tires are developed specifically for a new car and the difficulties encountered in testing tires on rough prototypes. Recently retired Viper plant manager John Hinckley and his assistant, Sylvia Holbert, both contributed more effort in assisting me than could have been reasonably expected.

Current and past members of the DaimlerChrysler PR staff, such as Dave Elshoff, Jan Zverina, and Tom Kowaleski, went to great lengths to provide the information and access needed to make this book better. Fellow members of the fourth estate generously recounted their Viper experiences for my benefit. Mike Allen, Matt Stone, and Bob Storck were each able to watch the Viper's development from close at hand, and their contributions were much appreciated. Particular thanks are due to Dan Ross, who provided valuable insight into the Viper's development and helped eliminate errors from this book before it reached your hands.

Peter Brock has been both a journalist and the designer of the Cobra Daytona Coupe, and his willingness to discuss his thoughts on the new coupe was very generous. Current and past presidents of the Viper Owners Club of America—Tony Estes, Steve Fergusen, and Maurice Liang—provided helpful observations from the community of fanatical owners that helped provide perspective on Viper ownership and motivations.

These acknowledgments only scratch the surface of the people with whom I discussed thoughts and recollections of the car's history, and if anyone has been excluded, I apologize.

Finally, I must thank my wife, Lynn, for her contributions to this book's completion. Her role may have been like Carroll Shelby's role as a catalyst in the Viper's development. Without her support in maintaining the household while I concentrated on writing, the book would not have happened.

—Dan Carney

CHAPTER ONE

A CONCEPT IS BORN

This is the type of sports car sketch that Chrysler's design department kept on the back burner even before the Viper project was approved. The long hood, flared fenders, and low-profile headlights and windshield are design cues that appeared in the concept car. *Matthew L. Stone*

In 1988, Bob Lutz, president of operations of Chrysler Corporation at the time, fretted over the Ford engine in his AC Cobra. He was a deep-rooted car guy and wasn't about to give up his Cobra, but the engine issue nagged at him. "The first thing I did when I got to Chrysler was remove the little 'Powered by Ford' plaque," he said. "I just took out the little pins and left the four holes in the car where the pins were."

With the Cobra sitting so conspicuously in Chrysler's parking lot, removing the plaque made it better, but not much. "I still felt a little disloyal about being a senior executive at Chrysler and driving a car that people who know something about cars associated with Ford," he said. So what he really wanted was a Cobra with a Chrysler engine. And, in a way, he got it. The 1992 Dodge Viper RT/10, the car that would launch an icon, grew out of those four little holes.

In the quarter-century since Carroll Shelby stuffed that first Ford small-block V-8 under the hood of an AC sports car, the Cobra legend had mushroomed. While Corvettes, Porsches, and Ferraris earned their due respect with sports car enthusiasts, the Cobra stood apart as a brutal weapon that made no concessions to comfort. It was an uncompromised, single-purpose, brute-force machine. Bob Lutz's kind of car.

9

"It was and is a cultural icon, in terms of expressing everything that a high-performance sports car is supposed to do," said Lutz. "It handles well. It's got a timelessly elegant, brutal appearance. It's got a great engine—there's nothing wrong with Ford V-8s—that sounds wonderful. The Cobra makes a statement. It's still a great car to drive."

Great as the Ford V-8 engine may have been, for Lutz it was still a politically incorrect engine.

The fact that the Viper ever saw the light of day owes itself to considerable serendipity, which is not to diminish the endless days and nights of hard, dedicated work by the members of what would become known as "Team Viper." But every journey begins with one step, and the first fortuitous step on the road to the Viper's birth was taken because, in 1988, Chrysler didn't make a strong V-8 engine. This was a cruel irony for the company that built the awesomely powerful and revered Hemi V-8. But the unfortunate reality was that there was no suitable Mopar engine to replace the Ford in Lutz's Cobra.

This concept exhibits heat extraction vents in the hood that are very similar to those on the production Viper. The abbreviated rally bar behind the cockpit hints at the eventual bar, and the red-and-yellow paint scheme made it to production. *Matthew L. Stone*

This is a more contemporary interpretation of the Viper concept. But even on this design, staples of Viper styling are present, including the rally bar, open trailing edges on the front fenders, and side pipes. *Matthew L. Stone*

This contemporary idea for the Viper appears to be a variation of the car above with more Viperlike squished headlights in place of the Porschelike round lights. This drawing saw the Viper as a pure convertible with no targa bar. *Matthew L. Stone*

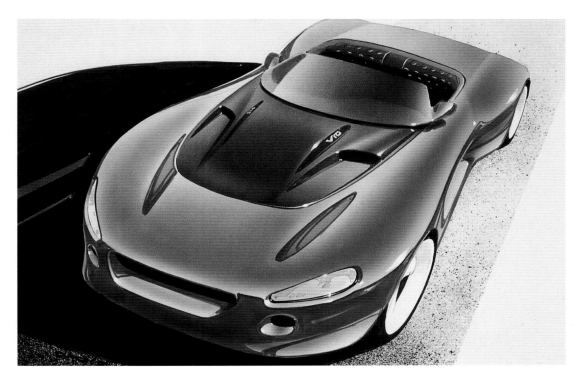

"At first I thought maybe I could get the 302 engine yanked out and substitute a Chrysler 360, which we were still making at that time for the Ram pickups," he said. "But we were making it without fuel injection and the horsepower was well below 200. So I would have had torque, but I wouldn't have had any real top-end performance. Nowadays the 360s develop 245 horsepower, and you can get parts from Mopar so that you can get it up close to 300 horsepower and still be emissions-legal."

But not back then. If the Mopar catalog had offered a decent performance engine in 1988, Lutz would have stuffed it into his Cobra and there probably never would have been a Viper. With Lutz's personal car problem solved, he would have moved on to worrying about how to solve Chrysler's many problems. As destiny would have it, solving Lutz's dilemma led to solving many of Chrysler's dilemmas, through nothing short of a company renaissance.

In mulling the issue at length, Lutz found himself considering outrageous possibilities.

"So I was driving along, and I thought, 'Wait a minute, we're going to have a cast-iron V-10 for the Ram pickup, and we're going to have a five-speed transmission,'" Lutz recalled, "a brand-new, New Venture Gear five-speed manual that was planned for the big pickup. So, I figured, you got the engine and transmission. You could probably use a lot of Dakota parts for front A-arms. If we want heavy-duty components and we were willing to go with a live rear axle, we could probably go with a Dakota rear axle. It could probably handle the torque.

"I thought, 'Gee, we really have all the parts'—maybe not yet in production, but we have enough parts in the parts bin coming—'that we could at least do a prototype,'" Lutz continued. "The next day I sat down with Francois Castaing and Tom Gale and said, 'Listen, here's my idea.'"

Viper stylists were thinking of the blue-and-white Cobra Daytona even before the Viper concept was built. Those colors reached production on the 1996 Viper GTS Coupe. This concept is close to the Viper in its rear styling, but the front end looks a bit more like a Corvette. *Matthew L. Stone*

If Chrysler had had the potential to build a decent performance vehicle without having to start virtually from scratch, it surely would have. But because it built only K-car derivatives and obsolete trucks, the desperation of the situation mandated a dramatic solution. A healthier company wouldn't have needed to build the Viper. Count Chrysler's ill financial health in the late 1980s as a necessary ingredient in the Viper's creation.

"Francois was only in charge of truck engineering at the time," Lutz said. "I knew if I dealt with the car guys I was going to get no cooperation because they were always too busy. They could never do anything. Francois said, 'We don't actually have a running V-10 yet; but that's no problem, we'll just take two 360s, cut them up, weld them together, and fabricate a crank. It won't be a great engine, but we can do a V-10 engine that runs and looks good.' I said that's all we'll need for a concept car. Gale said, 'This is what we've been waiting for; I'll get the guys going on the clay right away.' And that was sort of it."

"The Viper idea came out of the first meeting between Lutz and I in his office, in the spring of 1988," Castaing remembered. "We were pursuing and reconfirming a project to design and produce the big, iron, 8.0-liter V-10 for the trucks at Chrysler. In the midst of a casual meeting, Bob and I started discussing the fact that we were soon going to have a big American engine and that we could think about doing a sports car like people used to do in the 1970s or late 1960s in Europe. That was when an Italian or British or Swiss company would come and buy powerful drivetrains from the U.S. and start doing grand touring cars around them, like DeTomaso, Bizzarini, Iso Rivolta, or Jensen. People like that. We kind of mused around the idea that one day we will find a way to do a GT car.

"Bob, who owned a Cobra, said that's exactly what we need to do. He called Tom Gale in and said we were going to do a concept car that will use the early prototype of the V-10 truck engine. He laid out for Tom Gale that it would be a Cobra-type simple car. Tom went on and assigned one of his designers to do what turned out to be the Viper. He showed the sketch to Bob and I, and we decided to confirm the fabrication of the concept car that was presented in January 1989 at the auto show."

This sketch captures the styling of the production Viper almost perfectly. While the dual racing-style flip-open gas caps didn't make it onto the rear fenders of the production roadster, one did make it onto the roof pillar of the GTS Coupe. *Matthew L. Stone*

This meeting wasn't the first time Lutz and Gale had kicked around the wistful idea of a new Cobra. "We had various conversations about wouldn't it be wonderful to do a car like a Cobra or something that had that kind of excitement, that kind of performance, that kind of imagery," said Gale. Most any two car enthusiasts at the time had similar conversations. But Lutz and Gale were no garden-variety car nuts. They had the means to do it.

As Apollo 13 Commander Jim Lovell observed about going to the moon, for NASA it wasn't magic, "We just decided to go." At Chrysler the birth of a mythical V-10 supercar would happen the same way. Lutz, Castaing, and Gale decided to stop talking about building a new Cobra and just do it.

"Finally, Bob asked me to step in his office," continued Gale. "In just a five-minute meeting, he said, 'Why don't we just consider it?' It still wasn't necessarily an assignment, but it was far more serious than any discussion we'd had before. So as a result of that meeting, I had kicked it off.

"We were talking about a car that would be an icon."

Above

In the resource-scarce Chrysler Corporation, it wasn't clear the company would be able to execute its plan to build the V-10 Viper in a timely and cost-effective manner. This car could be called "Plan B." It is theV-8–powered 9/10ths-scale version built by the Pacifica design studio.

Left

If necessary, Chrysler could have built this smaller, lighter Viper, using the V-8 engine already in production. It's almost impossible to tell in the photos that the car is smaller than the real Viper.

The rear-end treatment of the Pacifica prototype is virtually identical to that on the original production cars.

Car designers are exactly as we imagine them. While they are supposed to be designing the next people-moving box on wheels, they find time to dash off sketches of their version of how a modern supercar should look. It's like 11th-grade study hall. As a result, more than a few killer sports cars were already doodled into notebooks.

So when Lutz gave Gale the go-ahead on the Viper concept car, Gale just so happened to have a few promising drawings lying around the design studio. "This gave me a chance to legitimize some of the work we had been doing," said Gale.

"Three weeks later, I came back to Bob with some half-scale packages of some of the work we had done," he said. "It was the basic packaging of the vehicle. It was a frame and body vehicle. It was a V-10. It was a set-back front/midengine layout where it had truly heroic proportions and the kind of scale we had envisioned. The Viper's current scale is very close to what we had. We also had probably half a dozen or so sketches we had been noodling on, and the graphics were not dissimilar to how the first concept car would look. It was always reasonably clear where we were heading."

Racing to make the North American International Auto Show in Detroit in January 1989, Gale's design team was well on its way to having a full-scale clay model completed, just six weeks later. For secrecy's sake, the work was being done in a small shop in Madison Heights, Michigan, 8 miles from Chrysler's Technical Center in Highland Park. "It was a shop where we used to build a lot of our fiberglass models," said Gale. "I used it because it was a good quick way to keep it out of sight of the system and a way to get it done quickly outside.

"When I took Bob to see the model, I think he was really impressed," continued Gale. "And I think he was caught by surprise. We'd had discussions, but they were always more philosophical, and now he was kind of surprised we had done so much. He wasn't completely comfortable with the graphics of the front, which turned out to be a strong key feature of the car, but he was very supportive and very enthusiastic, as he always was."

The Pacifica prototype wore three-spoke wheels that also appeared on the production car, along with the massive disc brakes that fill the insides of the wheels.

The impractical exposed header pipes didn't make it to production, but they sure looked good on the concept car and prototypes.

"I wasn't too fond of the design at first," admitted Lutz. "I thought it should be more reminiscent of the Cobra. But when I later saw it at MetalCrafters—and the first one was made out of metal—once I saw the real thing, I was just like everybody else. I was just blown away."

"Bob was always that way about styling, whether it was Viper, or in later years, things like the PT Cruiser, or whatever else," explained Gale. "He was always far more literal to the historic icon. That was one of the areas where we always tried to make it meet somewhere in the middle. We always had some pushing and pulling, but I think that's quite healthy."

"I don't believe we ever said it was going to be a Cobra," added Castaing. "It was going to be a modern sports car in the spirit of the Cobra; a roadster with a very powerful American engine. We were not trying to build a new Lamborghini Diablo. The car was going to be very simple, like a Cobra. Bob was adamant and I supported that, that the car should be like a new evolution of the Cobra."

The styling wasn't the only aspect of the car that Lutz originally planned to imitate the Cobra. Chrysler's latter-day Cobra might actually have been given the Cobra name, but for Ford's lawyers, who ultimately contributed to a happier ending. Dodge's icon surely deserved to establish its own legend with an original name, rather than be considered the latest chapter in the Cobra story.

"We worked on the name on an airplane trip back from the West Coast," Lutz recalled. "The marketing guy wanted to call it Dodge Challenger. We said, 'Aw, Christ, we're not going to do that.' What we really wanted was *Cobra*. Carroll Shelby thought he could get ownership of the name back from Ford, but it turned out he couldn't."

But the idea of a snake name, to reaffirm the car's Cobra inspiration, stuck. "We said, 'Hell, there are other snakes around.' But we weren't going to call it the Python or Boa Constrictor or Asp. 'How about *Viper*? Yeah, that's it: *Viper*.' "

Neither Lutz, Gale, nor Castaing claims to have suggested the name *Viper* first. They agree that the name was the result of a joint brainstorming session. "I don't know who said it first, whether I said it first, or Tom said it first, or Francois said it first," said Lutz. "But one of us said it first, and the rest of us said, 'Oh yeah, absolutely, let's talk to the trademark guys immediately and get that one locked up.'

Like most aspects of the original Viper, the logo was created quickly, with out debate or discussion.

"Then one of the guys in design got so inspired he immediately sketched an emblem with a grinning snake. It was spontaneous. It wasn't like, 'Well, we'll have a contest and we'll look at 15 emblems to pick one that we like, or why don't we take the shape of this emblem and incorporate the snake from that one.' There wasn't any of that. That grinning snake just appeared spontaneously, and we all said, 'Wow, that's it!' It all just came together with blinding speed."

Such synchronicity helped drive the Viper toward its date with destiny at the 1989 North American International Auto Show. "It was just a combination of the right bunch of guys with the right ideas in the right circumstances and a high degree of enthusiasm," said Lutz. "I wouldn't say never, but I think it's something that's seldom seen."

"In order to get the vehicle built we had to really run," said Gale. "There were not a lot of alternatives, which made it easier. There was one alternative and that was the way it was going to be, so we just ran headlong."

"We turned the project over to our West Coast Pacifica design studio," said John Herlitz, senior vice president of product design. "A young fellow by the name of Craig Durphy was responsible for the theme of the original roadster show car. From there we built the car from Craig's model."

"We didn't really show anybody a lot of the work," continued Gale. "We couldn't get the hardware we needed from engineering, so we had to make the parts and pieces we needed. We had to Siamese two cast-iron V-8s together to get a V-10. There was a lot of debate about whether we should do a somewhat smaller car, one that wasn't as aggressive in its packaging, that could be a V-8 instead of a V-10 car. So I built a 9/10th-scale version of the car. Nobody would know unless they measured it. We built that car at Pacifica in late 1988, and we actually had a hard model. That's why you'll see there was one car that had a sport cap and one car that didn't. There were early cars that were slightly different.

"The Pacifica model didn't expose very much. For all intents and purposes it had the final graphics, the final wheel design. The original three-spoke wheel came from that particular car. Those were all things that were trying to answer questions. We were trying to take off-line anything that was in question. By that late in the year I couldn't push and pull on the car we were going to have for Detroit, or I wasn't going to have anything for Detroit in January.

"It was never a particularly pretty thing, the original car. It could have used more development. But it got the job done. It ran, it moved. It filled the bill for being a benchmark concept vehicle back then."

It ran, it moved, it filled the bill. It got the job done.

Definitely, it got the job done. In fact, said Lutz, "The response to the show car was overwhelming. There wasn't a magazine in the States that didn't have it on page one."

Car nuts weren't the only ones who saw the Viper on all those magazine covers. Influential people, such as Wall Street analysts, whose comments could send Chrysler's stock spiraling downward, noticed the impact the Viper had, along with the bankers who controlled the company's financing.

"I had one Wall Street analyst call me up," said John Herlitz. "He had seen the car on the cover of one of the buff books and he said, 'John, just tell me you are going to build that car! You have to build that car!' "

CHAPTER TWO

BUILD IT!

At the time of the 1989 Detroit show, Chrysler was known as the K-car company. It suffered low esteem with customers after a succession of products based on that early-1980s' platform. The K-car was competent for its time, but characteristics—ride, handling, performance, and quality—that were acceptable for an economy sedan at that time were woefully inadequate later in the decade, in models with sport and luxury pretensions. Maybe the Dodge Aries didn't look too bad when compared to the cramped Toyota Corolla or Honda Civic of 1980, but the Dodge Daytona sport coupe, based on the same platform, couldn't hold a candle to the Acura Integra, which was based on a Honda Civic platform that was generations removed from the 1980 car. The company's family sedans fared no better against more modern, comfortable, and reliable Tauruses, Camrys, and Accords. For too long, Chrysler had been turning to its stylists to disguise the ancient car underneath. The only derivative of that platform to achieve significant acclaim was the minivan. But the minivan was more a triumph of market research than engineering, and it added nothing to Chrysler's rusty reputation for engineering excellence.

"The K-car was great in its time, but we just wore out that poor old platform," said design vice president John Herlitz. "It had become way obsolete in the marketplace. We had Spirit R/Ts, and that was about as hot as we got in those days."

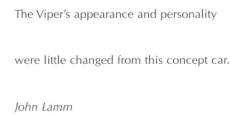

The Viper's appearance and personality were little changed from this concept car.

John Lamm

Added Bob Lutz, "You have to remember what a fundamentally demoralized company Chrysler was at that point. We had nothing but front-wheel-drive cars, we had no excitement, we had no car in the inventory with any more than a pushrod V-6 engine. Everything was a version of the K-car.

"The automotive press was giving us a beating. We were having trouble raising money because bankers would say, 'We're told by your competitors that there is no engineering capability left at Chrysler.' We had lots of engineering capability. But we only had one platform and two engines. It was just depressing."

"The idea with the Viper was to do something that was really a take-no-prisoners design statement for the Dodge division," said Herlitz, "and to reinvigorate the Dodge product line."

The Viper had already reinvigorated the Chrysler design staff, if not yet the Dodge product line. "Having been on the trailing edge of design for so many years, this was a great shot in the

The Viper concept car's Spartan dashboard accurately forecast the style and layout of the eventual production car's interior, with only a few detail differences. *John Lamm*

arm for the sense of camaraderie of the group," said Herlitz. "It was like a set of epaulets everyone could put on and strut proudly with—you can actually win the war with good design and great engineering. We were working on a car which in one fell swoop would have the highest number of cylinders in any American car produced since World War II and be the most expensive American production car in history. And not only the fastest American production car, but arguably right up there with the world's fastest high-performance cars like Lamborghini, the big Ferraris, and the Porsche Turbo."

As Herlitz had seen it, the Viper concept car took no prisoners, made a statement, and was a smash hit. Letters—some with deposit checks—were pouring in from would-be Viper buyers. But still that wasn't enough. Chrysler now had to make the difficult business decision as to whether it should—if even it could—build a production Dodge Viper.

The hand-built prototype V-10 didn't look exactly like the production unit, but it conveyed the impact of the Viper's massive engine. *John Lamm*

The V-8 option was simply a matter of expediency for a company in Chrysler's financial condition at the time. No one really wanted to exercise that option, least of all Lutz, who was passionate in his belief that a Viper would have to do Corvette one better, and the best way to do that would be with a V-10. Another reason to do the V-10 was to gird the Viper for battle against a daunting opponent: the legend of the Cobra. Over the years, the Cobra's performance reputation had grown to the point where it virtually defied the laws of physics. The challenge for Team Viper was not to build a faster car than the original Cobra, but to build a better car than enthusiasts remembered the Cobra to be. This was no small challenge.

"In the mind's eye, those cars were perfect," said Gale, who likened the Cobra's image to that of a high school girlfriend. "Looking back, we always remember her as absolutely gorgeous, intelligent, courteous. Everything a perfect person could be. And that's how the Viper had to be.

"But we still didn't know if we were going to build it. We didn't know if we were going to sell it. We didn't know if we were going to convince Lee Iacocca to go for it."

After the Detroit show, the tide to build the car was spreading as well as rising. Said Gale, "The reaction at the show really got it rolling. A lot of people in the company got convinced once we saw the response from the show car. It suddenly had more sponsors. We had discussions with lots of people, and there were more people involved. Francois Castaing did a great job of pulling people together. Everybody got behind it. Everybody loved it. People loved to come back with the things you'd asked them to fetch. They were proud to do it. It was a great process and it worked very well. The Viper wouldn't be here today if it weren't for getting all those people on board."

"We had never really intended to build the car," said John Herlitz, "but with that kind of reaction, there has got to be a way. We said, 'We just have to do this.'"

Lutz, Gale, and Castaing formed what would become the Viper Technical Policy Committee, which kept the car from 'going corporate' and being watered down. Said Gale, "The committee was to make sure we could monitor the progress, but it was more important to make sure the team was an assemblage of enthusiasts. It wouldn't matter if they were convicts; if they were pointed in the right direction we'd go for it. It was trying to get people who were really enthusiastic. But sometimes with that much enthusiasm, you have to make sure it was still going in the direction you wanted it to.

"At first there was myself, there was Francois, and there was Bob. Then we started to bring in others. Carroll Shelby was a part of that; he was certainly part of the spirit, and we wanted him on board."

But of course Lutz, Gale, and Castaing couldn't make the decision to build a Viper production car alone. They needed the money to do it, and Chrysler Chairman Lee Iacocca held the checkbook.

It was a skinny one in 1989, so they knew it would be difficult to convince any auto chief in his right mind to spend big money to build a radical sports car.

"The company was not doing very well," said Castaing. "Seventy million dollars was a lot to invest. A lot of people in finance and others were questioning whether our people were able to do a car like that. So we had to get the car blessed by Lee Iacocca, but he was a little bit uneasy about it. He had tried to do a similar project with DeTomaso three years earlier with the TC by Maserati, which turned out to be huge fiasco. And we were coming with a project he had not initiated himself. It was touchy."

Fortunately, Viper "four-father" Shelby was one of Iacocca's buddies from their Mustang days together at Ford.

"This is where Carroll Shelby really delivered," said Lutz. "Shelby and Iacocca were good friends. Iacocca trusted Shelby. One of the great advantages of bringing Shelby into it was that he would be a stronger voice with Iacocca than those of us inside the company would be."

So Lutz scheduled a meeting with Shelby and Iacocca. Said Lutz, "He basically sold Lee on it, told him, 'This is a great deal, you've got to do this, the car's going to be great.'"

Shelby's recollection of the meeting, typically, is colorful. "I said, 'I'll go talk to Iacocca,' because he had been turning us down for a long time," said Shelby. "He had turned me down on a sports car before Lutz got there. So we bullshitted him that we could do it for about $20 million. He OK'd it, but I had to meet with him and tell him we were on budget—until we got enough money in it he couldn't back out. That's what happened."

The Viper concept car's squatter styling is emphasized in this shot. For production, the windshield was more upright, and the car's lights and bumpers had to meet federal standards. Notice the curious sideview mirrors that are faired into the ends of the windshield. They persisted on some of the prototypes but disappeared prior to production. *John Lamm*

Left
Roy Sjoberg may not have been tagged as one of the Viper's "four-fathers," but he was certainly a founding father of the car. He steered the Viper through the maze from concept to production and into dealers' showrooms instead of history's dustbin. The experience from his years working with Corvette was priceless.

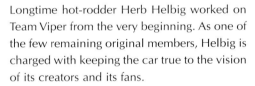

Longtime hot-rodder Herb Helbig worked on Team Viper from the very beginning. As one of the few remaining original members, Helbig is charged with keeping the car true to the vision of its creators and its fans.

Top right
Zora Arkus-Duntov, known as the "Father of the Corvette," also influenced the Viper's development, through Roy Sjoberg's pre-Viper apprenticeship on the Corvette program. Duntov attended the Viper's press launch gala, along with retired racers Phil Hill and Sam Posey. *John Lamm*

The real trick in convincing Iacocca to build the Viper was to let him drive it. Team Viper loaded the prototype up and carried it to the company's headquarters in Highland Park. After a turn at the wheel, Iacocca exclaimed, "What are you waiting for? Get this thing built!"

The real cost to develop the Viper from concept to production varies between $50 million and $75 million, depending on whom you ask. The $50 million number was the original target, and as more money was needed it became clear that it would be a good investment. The Viper was worth whatever it ultimately cost.

Employing the flair for drama that he used to win government loan guarantees and to personally pitch the company's cars on television, Iacocca staged the announcement of his approval for the Viper for maximum effect. On May 18, 1990, he stood before an audience of auto writers in Los Angeles and dramatically threw Lutz a set of keys. "Build it!" he cried.

Said Roy Sjoberg, Team Viper's new executive engineer, "The Viper would be our way of showing we were breaking out of the mold."

Sjoberg explains how he got the job as chief engineer. "Lutz and Castaing were trying to figure out who knew anything about sports cars around Chrysler, and who potentially knew how to execute such a project. I was the only guy."

Sjoberg had come to Chrysler from GM, where he had worked for years on the Corvette. His own mentor was no less than the great Zora Arkus-Duntov, father of the Corvette. Sjoberg brought more than experience on a similar project with him—he brought his Rolodex.

"The biggest thing was that Roy had the foundation in that sort of technology and was able to bring it to play quickly, with confidence, and not chase around dead-end solutions," said Bob Storck, a racer, engineer, and writer who watched Sjoberg push the Viper through its gestation

High-performance cars suffer a disproportionate number of single-car crashes, so Sjoberg built the Viper with survival in mind. Such rigorous standards and testing enhanced the Viper's reputation.

period. "Too often in an engineering group, you have a big variety of opinions. The manager who makes things happen is the guy who cuts through the clutter and moves forward without spending a lot of time and money on unproductive pursuits. I think that was the real benefit of getting Roy Sjoberg in there."

Sjoberg agreed. "I learned how do you do a low-volume niche vehicle in a large corporation, how do you deal with a bureaucratic structure and avoid some of the bureaucracy that really slows projects down, at least low-volume projects. I learned a lot of dos and don'ts and how you execute small teams. We did things that otherwise weren't possible to achieve. We did them in spite of General Motors."

One of the problems with small, specialized teams is that they are viewed as virtual outcasts in their companies, according to Sjoberg. "Small-team members in a large corporation are not loved," he said. "That is why Kelly Johnson [famed Lockheed airplane designer who created the P-38 fighter and U-2 and SR-71 spy planes] came up with the term *Skunk Works*. You're really a skunk in the corporation. People avoid you. On the Corvette, it was such that if the Corvette did something, no one else wanted to do it.

"Corvette did the first RIM (reinforced injection molding) fascia, for example. No one in the corporation wanted to do it, so they tried some other tack. Corvette was the first one to have a composite leaf spring. No one wanted to touch it in the corporation. It was kind of tainted if it had been introduced on the Corvette. And yet, what a great way to introduce new concepts, in low volume, minimizing the risks."

Lee Iacocca was known for his personal involvement with projects, as well as his dedication to particular concepts, and this was worrisome. Said Sjoberg, "The Chrysler Town and Country, which was Lee's idea for an all-leather minivan, we all knew that was a dumb idea; but he pushed it through. For some reason, he knew the Town and Country was right, and he stayed involved, pushing.

"On the Viper, I guess he knew he didn't know enough about it, and he stayed uninvolved. He left me alone. He just said, 'OK, what do you need?' I told him, and he said, 'You got it. Get outta here.'

"He only visited us three times, but he was always supportive. He was the guy that gave me the 50 million bucks, which was paramount. Without having a purse of money, if I had had to go on my hands and knees to somebody monthly or quarterly, like many of the projects at that time at Chrysler, the Viper would have died. I had watched that, working on the Corvette. We'd go in for money and the Camaro guys would be right behind us saying, 'Hey, for that kind of money we can sell 10,000 more Camaros, and they aren't going to sell another Corvette.' As soon as they'd make that argument, we'd lose the money. So I had learned. When I went to Iacocca I said, "I need $50 million and I need it as a chunk.' And he was willing to do that."

But now Team Viper needed a home. Sjoberg had been looking for space for his people for some time. "We were working primarily out of a warehouse the first couple [of] weeks," he recalled. "Then one of our mechanics noticed that the Jeep design staff was moving out of its area at Jeep/Truck Engineering, so I called Trevor Creed, who was director of Jeep/Truck, and asked if it was true. He told me to keep it quiet because no one knew they were moving. Well, we're not lawyers or anything, but they say possession is nine-tenths of the law, so we moved in that night."

The project's can-do spirit was building up steam. The team needed to equip its new space, so they looked around the company for available tools. They needed basic items such as computers, dyno cells, and vehicle lifts. "We didn't steal anything from other groups," said Sjoberg. "We just used good intelligence to find out when equipment was being underutilized, then asked if we could borrow it. We did a lot of good, old-fashioned horse-trading to get some of our tools. We all knew we had limited people and we had to empower them. And we all knew whatever money we had, we had to give it to the car, and then give it our all and risk it."

"The guys who invented that car are incredible heroes," said Peter Brock, designer of the Shelby Cobra Daytona Coupe. "They put their careers on the line, they took jobs with lesser pay to work on that program. And they created that thing with their own intensity—a lot of long hours and a lot of their own time, stealing from other programs in the company to make it happen."

The daunting mission of the Viper Team was to produce an exciting car, with little budget and little development time. Said Francois Castaing, "We wanted the team to be very fast, very unbureaucratic, very effective to make sure the car would be produced on time to cut corners on the paperwork and bureaucracy that are sometimes part of a big company.

"We were looking at keeping the price below $50,000, which was very low for a powerful car like that, so we had to be very disciplined about the content of the car," he added. "Lutz and I were adamant that the car would stay simple like the Cobra. It would be rudimentary, but it would be brute force. It would be extremely fast; it would be spectacular to look at. For the sake of making the car different and keeping the price low, it was designed to have no frills, no moving windows, no ABS brakes, things that a side of the company could not comprehend we weren't looking at. So the issue of the content of the car kept coming back."

Sjoberg put it into perspective by putting some words from Bob Lutz on a pedestal: "I thought the best statement Bob Lutz ever said was, 'Gentleman, what we need are cars that are not just nice cars. What we need are cars that one out of three people hate, one out of three doesn't know what it is, and one out of three people absolutely has to buy it. If we can get one-third of the market, of people who absolutely have to buy our cars, we are a home run. If all three people say, 'It's a nice car,' we've got ho-hummers and we haven't got a chance. We can't compete with the GM buying power; we can't compete with the Ford marketing power. We're just the third guy on the rung here. We've got to have products that they pound our doors down to buy."

Castaing continued the development story. "I asked Roy Sjoberg to convene a monthly Viper technical policy committee meeting, and these meetings were bringing up issues such as the size of the fuel tank, using gearbox A versus gearbox B, things like that. So we were having good discussions together and helping Sjoberg move along. When he had choices, he would talk to us, or if he was going in a direction that was making me or someone else uncomfortable, we would discuss it."

Castaing was made uncomfortable by Sjoberg's insistence on the RT/10's "rally bar," which would detract from the smooth top-down profile. "The bar was my requirement, and Francois and I went around and around on this several times," said Sjoberg. "He did not care for it. I felt strongly it should have it on. That was from my experience on the Corvette. A lot of the accidents involving high-performance two-seat sports cars are single-car accidents from off-road excursions. The driver tries to get back on the road too fast and trips it.

"The bar was always there as a consideration, not a prime protector, but a consideration for rollover protection. We never said it was a rollover bar, because it isn't. It's not at the right height.

"Viper VM01 didn't have the structure. It made it easier and quicker to build. VM02 had the bar, and every vehicle thereafter had the bar."

The V-10 engine is now an article of faith, but in the beginning there was even disagreement among its creators about the wisdom of using such a big engine. "I would have liked to have built a 2,800-pound car," said Shelby, "but when you put a V-10 in there, you don't have a chance. You gotta have big halfshafts and a big gearbox, a lot of mass there to handle the torque."

Accepting such debates as a healthy part of the process, the group met regularly to gauge progress and chart the future. The meetings also let Castaing test the mettle of the team members and ensure the right people were on the team. "That was a way for me to assess whether the volunteer group that Roy put together had all of the talents that were necessary to conduct the project. I helped bring in new people when I found out they were struggling with one aspect of the car because Roy was short of a couple [of] specific professionals. We didn't replace people on the team when they were lacking some experience. We would bring people from the big group to help."

One of those people was Herb Helbig, who is the only original member of Team Viper still with the program. He is now manager of vehicle synthesis. Helbig's hot-rod roots run deep. He grew up

The Viper name embossed on the V-10's valve cover is now legendary, but early in the development process the use of a V-10 engine was seriously questioned. Its use drove a series of decisions about other components, such as the transmission and the brakes. *John Lamm*

street-racing 1956 and 1957 Corvettes he built himself, and later a flathead Hi-boy roadster. In 1998 he ran a Viper Coupe on the dry lakes, setting a record of 180 miles per hour at Muroc.

"We had a direct line to the very top of the company," he recalled. "This was a big help in keeping us focused and keeping the naysayers away. Lutz, Castaing, Gale, and Shelby were on a first-name basis with virtually everyone on the team. We had access to senior management that no other platforms had because we were small and because we were, quite frankly, doing Bob's favorite project. I used to call him every Friday afternoon, which was great. He was the champion of our team."

Other potential adversaries to the Viper were kept at bay by the knowledge that it was Lutz's pet project, according to Herlitz. "There was not a single bean counter who got in the way because they knew it was Lutz-driven, so they rolled with it," he said. "Otherwise they'd have been in the studio stopping everything. I've been in this business for 37 years, and I've seen a lot of projects that came to a screeching halt because the guy at the top didn't understand what the team was working on. Or the financial boys got in the way with questions like, 'What are you wasting time on this stuff for when we've got production work to do?' Fortunately, that wasn't the way the Viper project worked out."

Such support made it easier to build the Viper, but it didn't pave the way. "Everything was a challenge," Helbig said. "The technical challenges were we were doing a brand-new car, a brand-new body technology, and we were building an engine from scratch. The three requirements were you've got to do it in 36 months, you've got to do it with $50 million, and you've got to be moral, ethical, and legal. Those were Bob's going-in rules. Beyond that, we could do pretty much whatever we wanted to do."

The limited budget, Lutz's original plan to turn a bunch of truck parts into a sports car, and the actual use of some existing parts such as a switchgear, have led to the Viper's early reputation as a parts-bin special. But that's more folklore than truth, according to Helbig. Maybe even wishful thinking, given the tight budget.

"There was some parts sharing, but not a hell of a lot," he said. "Let's face it, we didn't have a lot of sports car parts lying around on the shelves at Chrysler Corporation in 1989. We might have used a parking brake mechanism. I think we shared a rear brake caliper. We shared the pickup truck wheel hub assembly, which is how we got six studs in the first place. We said, 'Yeah, that's cool; it'll work for us.'"

So the jokes about Viper rolling along on truck parts are at least founded in truth, but the cracks about it having a truck engine aren't. Lutz's original plan may have been to use the truck engine, but it didn't exist when Team Viper was working on its engine. "Oh, there were some lines on paper about building a truck V-10," said Helbig, "but an iron-block V-10 in a car like the Viper wasn't going to get it because of the weight. That's a formula for failure."

In the end, the Viper shared only the same number of cylinders, with Chrysler tapping Lamborghini for help on the aluminum block, head, and other components.

The Dodge Viper had hit Chrysler like a boulder dropped in a wading pool. A shock wave was felt throughout the company. It would ultimately affect how other products were developed, the company's attitude toward risk, the morale of its employees, and customers' opinions of the company.

CHAPTER THREE

BUILDING IT

The Viper RT/10 as it appeared in 1992, complete with three-spoked wheels. The headlights, which had been mounted in the hood clamshell in the concept car and prototypes, have been mounted directly to the car. When they were attached to the hood, they vibrated excessively. *John Lamm*

The Viper might have ended its life as a styling exercise. Or as a prototype that never got built, lost in the land of wild ideas. Or it might have been a boutique halo car—a halo car produced under contract by an outside supplier. Clearly, it was a halo car, built purely (from an economic standpoint), but importantly, for image. The minivan shines in the Viper's glow. Draws 'em into the showrooms.

Chrysler had been down the halo-car road before. But unlike the Viper, the TC by Maserati was a semiboutique halo car, assembled by Maserati using Chrysler components. It provided none of the benefits of in-house development, as the Viper did. It was doomed to failure because its intentions were impure—and that was so very different from the Viper. The TC was supposed to be an image machine, but when it looked in the mirror it saw a K-car chassis. There was something a bit too desperate about trying to pass off a K-car as an image machine. Few, if any, were fooled. It didn't help that the TC was as poorly executed as it was ill-conceived.

"It was extremely expensive and never brought any positive PR to the company," said Sjoberg. " It turned out to be a way to ridicule the company in the end.

31

"Because of the problems we were having at the time, and because DeTomaso was a friend of Lee Iacocca's, we chose to try to create a Maserati TC. But for less money you could have a LeBaron convertible. It was really a marketing debacle and it was a production-quality debacle. There wasn't much to be learned engineering-wise.

"I was in charge of materials for Chrysler Corporation during the TC. Most of our problems were DeTomaso problems, and Maserati's insufficient facilities. I wouldn't have painted a Yugo in the Maserati paint shop. Ferrari felt so strongly about it that when Ferrari got Maserati, they ripped it all down. They brownfielded the whole area. There's only one assembly building left at Maserati and one relatively new engineering building, but otherwise they're starting from scratch."

He continued, "Most people knew the TC was bad news and stayed away from it. Even though I had paint responsibility, I knew how bad it was, so I never went to Maserati. I stayed away from it.

"The TC was a loser from day one. It didn't teach us anything."

With a green light for production, Team Viper first built a pair of prototypes. Prototype VM-01 (white) still had no rally bar. VM-02 (red) looked much like the concept car but with a taller windshield. *Matthew L. Stone*

Chrysler wasn't the only company that made this mistake.

"Remember the Cadillac Allante?" asked Bob Lutz. "That was obviously a completely failed effort because that was GM's version of Chrysler's TC by Maserati. It was ugly, it was heavy, it had no redeeming social value. It was Italian, but it didn't look Italian. I don't think that car did anything for the Cadillac image."

Although the Italian coach-builder approach to sports car design and assembly didn't work for Chrysler, or for GM later, it taught Chrysler some lessons that helped the company succeed with the Viper. The unloved TC might be appreciated for contributing to the Viper cause.

Team Viper could claim to be more than just another pretty halo. It was a corporate prototype in itself. Because the Viper was being built very quickly and with a very tight budget, it took a lot of new ideas to keep going. Team Viper's creativity in speeding the car's development was a new game. Everything was open to change. New approach? Fine. Our assignment is to make it up as we go along. Management, contracts with suppliers, new technology—everything.

Said Tom Gale, "The Viper project was more about being a prototype for how we were going to manage the company, going forward. This was one of the first platforms. Here was this group of people who were working in a very different way, that had a lot of sponsorship in the company. It was literally the prototype for what we did. The car was a wonderful experiment. There was some of that going on from a pure management perspective. It really was the prototype for the way we later reorganized the company into platforms."

Added Herb Helbig, manager of Viper synthesis, "One of the premises of the Viper was that it was an opportunity to try out technology in low volume. It was one of the things that drove the decision to use plastic body panels. Part of Viper's heritage today is to look at technology where it makes sense in low-volume applications.

"We have a plastic deck lid on the Sebring convertible now," Helbig added. "That kind of stuff trickles over. We put power adjustable pedals in the Viper. That allowed us to do a better job fitting drivers to Vipers. Now we are going to see adjustable pedals on some of the larger-volume platforms. That's something that we started. In fact, *Good Housekeeping* magazine gave us an award for our adjustable pedals. That's not exactly the kind of magazine that you'd think would give an award to a 400-horsepower sports car."

As it built the Viper, Chrysler was remaking itself in the Viper's image. Certainly cars that followed bore no resemblance to the K-car. Viper served as a model for platform teams for Chrysler, in which the company's departments and disciplines work on the car simultaneously and together. Previously, each department took its turn with the design; traditionally, each department accomplished its objectives at some expense to the next. The car that appeared at the end of the line was often a far cry from the car that began the process.

As executive engineer, Sjoberg recruited allies within Chrysler, people on other teams, promising that if they helped Team Viper they would be rewarded with new concepts and technologies they could later use on their cars. "One thing we did on Team Viper, at all times, was attempt to keep the large corporation interested in the project," said Sjoberg. "We always made sure we had a sponsor in large-car platforms or truck platforms that really wanted to execute whatever creative idea we had, if it worked and if it proved out."

Looking back, it seems astonishing that Team Viper was also building a radical new engine from a nearly clean sheet of paper, to a deadline pace. Ruling out the truck engine meant the team members had to build what they wanted themselves.

The body of prototype VM-01 goes onto the frame on a level table to ensure correct alignment. *Daniel Charles Ross*

With the body installed, Team Viper members tweak and sand VM-01's plastic. *Daniel Charles Ross*

The V-8 engine has been dropped into VM-01. VM-02 would use an iron-block V-10, but that engine wasn't available for VM-01. Notice the stamped steel suspension arms. These Dakota truck parts were quickly deemed unsuitable for the production Viper. *Daniel Charles Ross*

Said Francois Castaing, "It was already April 1989. If we wanted the car to be ready by January 1992, we needed to really get going. But the timing for the truck engine was a year later. It also became obvious, when we looked at it more thoroughly, the weight of the iron engine was too high and the power we would get from it wouldn't be sporty enough."

Said Roy Sjoberg, "We rapidly ascertained, the truck guys and myself, that where we wanted a 6,200-rpm redline, the truck guys didn't really care to go over 4,200 rpm. They were interested in low-end torque, not horsepower at high-rpm levels where we were. They were not concerned about weight. Truckies don't like aluminum blocks. They're not as forgiving, and truck people like to have things that are pretty bulletproof.

"Not a lot could be learned from our truck V-10 development. Both engines were V-10s, but one was aluminum and one was iron; ours was sequential-fire individual-injected, and the truck's was group-injected, so it ended up having air pumps and things. We only needed EGR to meet the initial emission requirements, as well as a catalyst. The truckers had to put some other things on it. We ended up with the same dimension pushrod and that was it. But even there, we used a higher-grade material because of our power and rpm requirements."

In the end, there wasn't a single shared part with the Ram V-10 that was being built elsewhere within Chrysler.

As the notion to use the truck engine quickly faded, Team Viper went through a nervous period asking "Now what?" Said Castaing, "Bob Lutz was very anxious for the car to proceed, so he said maybe we can use the 5.9 V-8 instead. I said, 'No, no, no, the V-10 is so magic as part of this car. We have to find a way to do an engine, even if it is a derivative of the truck engine. We have to explore a way of doing that.'

The proportions of the finished VM-01, with its taller DOT-legal windshield, seemed wrong. The car also lacked side pipes, foreshadowing the 1996 models with rear exhaust.

VM-01 was far from the car's production version, but Team Viper was proud to pose with the car that represented so much inspiration, vision, creativity, faith, promotion, engineering, and plain hard work.

It didn't take long for Team Viper to discard the original plan to use the cast-iron truck V-10, because of the engine's sheer mass. So they built a densely packaged aluminum V-10 that, by its second generation, weighed 160 pounds less than the truck engine.

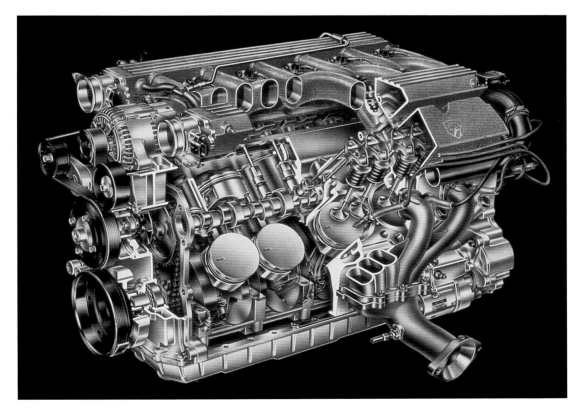

Team Viper collaborated with Lamborghini to convert the iron-block V-10 to an aluminum design. This wooden model shows the engine moving toward its final form, which shared no components with its iron-block cousin.

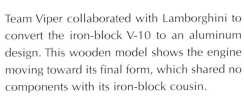

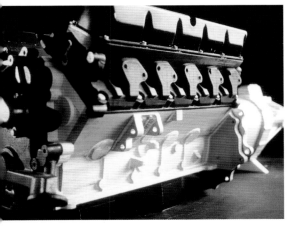

"I was convinced that if we didn't make too many mistakes, there was a chance for us to have a better engine, a very distinctive engine in the V-10 and not another pumped-up V-8 like in the Corvette. Over the course of the summer, finally, Bob Lutz, who was concerned that this was not cutting it timing-wise, started relaxing. Obviously the engine was way more powerful than a V-8, so it was good from that perspective. The engine turned out to be, in my view, part of the legend of the car. I'm glad we insisted at the beginning that it had to stay a V-10."

But the engine wasn't just part of the legend of the car, it *was* the car.

"At the time, we owned Lamborghini," he continued. "So I called them and said, 'I need your help to convert as quickly as we can the drawings of a truck engine into an aluminum design from a cast-iron design. And I want your very fast prototyping sources to produce a math casting so we can start prototyping an engine for the Viper as quickly as we can.'

"They agreed to do that, so [engine manager] Jim Royer took the design and flew to Bologna, Italy, where Lamborghini's Formula One team was. Lamborghini assigned a couple [of] engineers and a drafter, and they modified quickly the block design, a casting of the block and the head to make it more like a car engine."

But it wasn't that simple. "Lamborghini was an acquisition we had," Sjoberg said, "so Francois thought that perhaps Lamborghini could help us in converting an iron V-10 concept to aluminum, because they should know about those things. They were designing the basic individual components from iron to aluminum. Our contract with them was to produce five aluminum engines, our basic design. They were to deliver five engines, running. We ended up getting one set of engine parts, nonrunning. At that point we separated.

"They were very oriented to high rpm, not oriented to torque, but oriented to horsepower at high rpm," he explained. "But they were not so worried about produceability and not so worried about

This cutaway exposes how the Viper seems to be shrink-wrapped around its tremendous 8.0-liter V-10 engine, like a piston-engined fighter plane. The tubular steel space frame design let Team Viper build prototypes more quickly and simply.

Who would have believed that the production Viper would retain the muscular flared fenders and brash side pipes that were key elements of the concept car's design? An important change from the concept car was raising the windshield to a legal height, so drivers looked through—rather than over—the glass.

reliability, and I was very insistent that we were going to have an engine that met all the basic Chrysler Corporation engine life and durability requirements, both dynamometer and vehicle. They weren't worried about that at all.

"They wanted the engine to be sleeveless. There was no way I was going to have anything to do with any engine other than an iron-sleeved aluminum engine. When I was at General Motors, in one of my positions of infamy, I was the Vega cooling engineer. Vega had a sleeveless aluminum engine. Bore recession was the killer, and as for being forgiving for low coolant levels, it was absolutely a disaster.

"Lamborghini did help with the base concept of how to convert to aluminum. And they provided some aesthetics of the outward part of the engine, how it looks. But the components we got from them, we ended up redesigning substantially to assure adequate durability. They weren't worried about 300 hours of dynamometer durability at wide-open throttle. That wasn't their concern. So, yes, they helped us with some directional issues, but in the end, none of their components lasted and were totally redesigned."

The Viper's engine program had now gone in opposite directions: too much trucklike torque and not enough rpm or power in the Ram engine, and in the Lamborghini execution there was too much rpm and not enough torque or reliability. The Viper eventually found its middle ground between Clydesdale and Thoroughbred by Team Viper's simply doing it themselves.

"The largest obstacle was a business strategy process issue," said Sjoberg. "Finding the right suppliers. High performance, low volume is not something most suppliers are organized to do. But I found that they were very receptive to the idea of testing technologies on the Viper.

"Our biggest problem on that was the transmission," he continued. "We started out with ZF, and very early on we cut them off. It was too expensive. We could buy anything they made; they weren't oriented to design anything specifically for us.

"Then we moved to Getrag. They worked very hard to do design, but they were still European and they couldn't identify with the level of torque and horsepower our engine was going to put out. We never got durability with the Getrag and their costs kept going up and up."

Part of the problem was that it was a six-speed transmission. Only the T-56 transmission Borg-Warner was developing for GM seemed to fit the bill. The Corvette guys could have nixed any thoughts of letting Dodge share their transmission, but because Sjoberg had worked on the Corvette, he was able to persuade his old friends to cooperate on the project. "They wanted the competition," he said.

"We were very fortunate because of my working relationship on the Corvette and with Borg-Warner for many years. We were able to make a joint venture with Borg-Warner in concert with General

Motors to develop their six-speed transmission that they had started design and development on with General Motors for the Camaro and Firebird, which is now also used on the Corvette.

"At that time, the transmission head at GM was John Froning. He and I had worked on the Corvette together. Since Borg-Warner was tooling it, and it wasn't General Motors' money, John was receptive to the collaborative engineering and production effort with us on developing the six-speed.

"I knew GM would be more worried about NVH [noise, vibration, harness] and finesse. We were more worried about brute horsepower. They liked that idea, because they were going to have an engine down the road with more horsepower.

"They had their own case and we had our own case. It was a pretty uniform interior box. Borg-Warner did all the tooling for the gears. They owned the gears and we just bought them. As they made shift changes, we adapted to them. As we made power changes, they adapted to it. Getting Borg-Warner to sign up for that and understand what we wanted and our needs and our method of operating as a development group was a sizeable effort. But Borg-Warner worked real hard at it and really developed a mirror image of our Skunk Works inside Borg-Warner."

As if all these new things weren't enough, a progressive new marketing approach was in place. Journalists were not only shown the Viper's development, they were invited to

The speedometers on the first Vipers read to 180 miles per hour, and the car could mostly cash the checks the speedometer was writing. The numbers have since climbed to 200 miles per hour and to 220 miles per hour, and the car continues to be able to use most of the gauge's range. *John Lamm*

Sports cars traditionally had little more than a plank across the dash, with all the necessary gauges set into it. The Viper maintained the same feel, but with the requisite addition of HVAC vents and controls and a stereo system. *John Lamm*

production and engineering meetings. They were trusted to keep certain specifics under an embargo until the car was finished, but they were able to use enough material to keep the Viper continuously on their magazine covers.

"There were a bunch of us from the buff books that were at those Viper roundtables in the very early days," said Daniel Charles Ross, editor-in-chief of *Mopar Performance News*, who was *Motor Trend*'s national editor at that time. "That was the first time that had ever been done to such an extent, both in terms of information provided and the number of people they included. It was a broad number, not just the buff books, but the so-called 'screwdriver books,' with Jim Dunne. It was fascinating to be sitting around the table with folks and be talking with Helbig and Sjoberg and folks like that who were actually telling you the stuff they had probably done that day. We had never had, as a group, the unwashed journalist class, had never had that kind of collective exposure to such a program before."

Said veteran auto writer Bob Storck, "Obviously the thing was extremely limited in the beginning, with such things as no top and creature comforts. But I thought they did a good job of working all that in. They chose very simple but well-proven schemes like the standard ladder frame with deep section rectangular tubing. Not elegant, not light, but when you've got that 8-liter V-10 you can get away with a little bit.

"In contrast, look at the C5 Corvette and how they worked that up. The way you accomplish things in a sports car is to even the weight distribution and stiffen the center section of the car. In the C5, they were able to do that by shoving the transmission to the rear and building a big box for the driveshaft to go through, then having two big bulkheads, fore and aft, that were tied together by that box and by the hydro-formed side rails.

"The Viper, not having the ability to go through such an elegant piece of design, chose the ladder frame and tied that together with the roll-hoop, a big cowl bulkhead, a deep section around the transmission box, and big side rails. Getting in and out of the car you gave up some convenience, but it wound up accomplishing a lot of the same thing. It's just not as elegant."

The steel tube space frame is more typical of an older race car than of a sports car in series production, if not exactly mass production. Stamped steel unibody floorpans are the norm for modern cars, but they aren't as rigid, nor are they as easy to modify during development. The space frame also provided a nice bit of symmetry with the legendary sports and racing cars of old, such as the Shelby Cobras and Ferraris, not to mention the famous "birdcage" Maserati.

By December 1989, the team had built its first prototype, VM-01, using a V-8 engine. Only a couple of months later, in February 1990, the V-10–powered VM-02 was ready. Journalists were now able to get rides in the car. They couldn't drive it, but they could ride shotgun with Bob Lutz. *Automobile* magazine's founder and publisher, David E. Davis, a large presence with a strong and colorful voice within the industry, earned the privilege of the first ride. Unfortunately, the prototype had plastic doorsills, which began burning. The car came back smoking heavily on both sides. *Automobile* readers got a memorable column out of it.

"This was the initial prototype," said Sjoberg. "If your catalyst gets overheated, which it can if you race it hard, or if you have fouled plugs, you can get some substantial temperature. The sills did start to smoke. There weren't flames flying in the air, but it was obvious when you see that level of smoke, something was burning. So I just casually went into the tent and got two pitchers of water from the buffet table and came out and poured them on the sills."

TEST RIDE WITH LUTZ

Daniel Charles Ross, Mopar Performance News *editor-in-chief, recalls an eventful ride in a Viper prototype piloted by Bob Lutz:*

On that trip, there was just the one car and many were called to ride in it. The program was that you'd ride in the car with Lutz on legs established all the way up this mountain and down a driving route on the other side. When your stint in the car was over, you would be met at a waypoint by a shuttle vehicle that would take you on to the lunch stop. I was the second or third leg that morning. Lutz and I are old acquaintances, and so we had a lively conversation going.

We got to my waypoint and the person who was being shuttled to this point to take over my seat in the Viper wasn't there. We waited 10 minutes or so and Lutz said, "OK, time to go." So I got to go on two stints.

There is no top on this car—an RT/10—and the side exhausts were blaring and this was the car that was prototype, so the exhaust tuning wasn't final. I don't think it had any functioning instruments except the tach and the four across the top-center of the dash, where you got oil and temperature and so on. The speedo was not working, but the tach was.

The dash had a paper chart taped to it in the place where the HVAC and radio would go later. The chart gave an RPM figure at each certain gear that equaled so many miles per hour. We didn't pay very much attention to speed.

Lutz was just flying up the mountainside in this car, and the faster he went, the more wind buffeting there was. After a few minutes, with all the wind and exhaust noise, we didn't have much conversation. And on the second leg, it was getting fairly cold.

He had a small radar detector on the inside of the windshield, but it wasn't very effective in the mountains. We were on a twisty little two-lane and there wasn't much traffic, but every time there would be traffic, we would just fly around it, even on a couple of blind curves on the double-yellow.

At one point there was a long uphill run-up so Bob hammered on up there. We could see there was an '87 T-Bird Turbo Coupe up ahead of us. It was clear, by the way he was driving, that Lutz was going to take this car in the curve. We went flying past the thing and didn't look back.

I specifically looked at the tach when we went past the T-Bird and, according to the paper chart of rpm, we were doing approximately 138 miles per hour when we passed the T-Bird, and we just kept on going. Minutes later, we came down off the hilly portion and onto the valley portion where it is long and straight. We hear this really high-pitched whine. We both looked at each other, like, "What the hell is that?" I thought it was a leak in a heater hose. It sounded like a teakettle whistle.

Lutz looks in his mirror and here was this Turbo Coupe, it's got red-and-blue lights flashing in the grille, and as we've slowed down in the valley, it's caught up to the Viper—and I know that guy had to keep the Turbo Coupe's candle lit a long time to catch up with us. At the same time Lutz is pulling over to stop, he's scrambling to pull the radar detector off the dash. He threw it in my lap and I stuffed it under my seat.

The Turbo Coupe pulls over in front of us and this guy gets out in civilian clothes. When he got out in civilian clothes, in this kind of a car, I knew we were not going to be in too much trouble. But this guy was clearly pissed. So here he comes, big western-style shirt, with the pearl buttons and everything, and a big rodeo belt buckle of some kind.

As the guy comes up to the car, he is talking a blue streak, none of it is friendly, and he reaches for his wallet and flashes a badge. He is just screaming at Lutz, nearly blue-in-the-face stuff, about how he is a captain in the sheriff's department and you can't be drivin'—goddammit—around here like that and you passed me on the double yellow, and if I wasn't going somewhere else I'd call a car to give you a ticket right now!

When he said he was already headed somewhere else, I figured that meant we were home free. But Lutz was playing Mr. Diplomat to the hilt and being unbelievably apologetic. At the same time he's telling the guy three "I'm sorrys" a minute, he's telling the guy he's the vice-chairman of Chrysler, we're out here with this journalist group, maybe I got a little over-enthusiastic and all this stuff.

The cop just screamed at him for a couple [of] minutes. Didn't care what Lutz had to say, just that Lutz *heard* what he had to say. And he got in his Turbo Coupe and roared away.

Well, in the meantime, this young kid in a Honda has pulled over to watch this whole thing. Right next to us, right across the road from where we're pulled over. As soon as the Turbo Coupe pulls away, the kid jumps out of his car and he is all over Lutz.

Turns out he's the service tech at the local Dodge dealer and [this] was the first Viper he'd ever seen. Not only is he looking at the first Viper, he is talking to Bob Lutz! I thought the guy was going to pee in his pants when he found out it was Lutz driving the Viper. Talk about a doubleheader. It was like Lutz was a rock star. Lutz was very gracious and accommodating, gave the kid his card, told him, "If you guys ever need anything, call me personally."

That was the last stint before the lunch stop, and nothing exciting happened after that. ■

The leather-trimmed Viper interior turned out to be a surprisingly luxurious space, at least when the sun was shining. The large speakers mounted between the seats gave the Viper's stereo good sound, though the stereo may go largely unused by many drivers. *John Lamm*

The tale of the Viper's debut certainly contributes to the legend, but it accomplished something concrete. "It formalized the decision that we would use aluminum for the doorsills," deadpanned Sjoberg.

Corvette and Viper history intersected officially when Sjoberg invited Zora Arkus-Duntov, the father of the Corvette, to test a Viper prototype. Duntov had been Sjoberg's mentor when they were at GM, where Duntov had guided and driven the Corvette through its evolution from a striking but timid rookie sports car with a straight-six engine to a fire-breathing V-8 icon of its own. He invented and sold the first stripped-down and beefed-up Corvette street racer, the 1963 Stingray Coupe. The heritage continued with the 2001 385-horsepower Corvette Z06. The *Z0* stands for *Zora*, a tribute to the man who created the Corvette.

Sjoberg wanted to show off the Viper to his mentor, and when the idea of a visit from the retired Corvette boss was approved, he wasted no time in having Duntov come drive a Viper before its introduction. "One of my good memories was when Francois Castaing allowed me to invite Zora Duntov to come out to the proving grounds to drive the car," said Sjoberg. "He loved it."

"Zora was a tremendous driver at one time, but by then he was older and his driving skills weren't what they once were. So we spun once, but he liked the car.

"A lot of the time there was a bunch of the Viper team huddled around him," Sjoberg added. "Most of them got his autograph."

Sjoberg kept up with Duntov until Duntov's death in the mid-1990s. "Zora and I both loved martinis, and we got together once a quarter and told stories about Vipers and Corvettes," he said.

The enormous V-10 engine generates prodigious amounts of heat that need a way out from under the hood. The vents provide that outlet, and, well, they look cool too. *John Lamm*

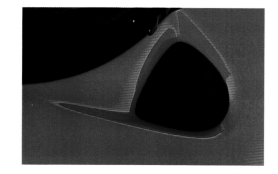

The Viper's rally bar provided a convenient spot for the government-mandated center high-mounted stoplight. *John Lamm*

As Duntov appreciated the Viper, Sjoberg remains a Corvette driver. He owns Viper street and racing cars, but he races a 1966 Corvette. "I can't go vintage racing with a Viper," he explained.

The Viper got some early good exposure at the 1991 Indianapolis 500. Chrysler had arranged to supply a pace car and had intended to use the Dodge Stealth V-6 turbo sport coupe. But it soon became apparent that this plan was flawed. The Stealth was built by Mitsubishi in Japan, and Chairman Iacocca was remembered for railing against Japanese automakers. Plus, Chrysler was a company that had recently been bailed out with loan guarantees from the American government.

The obvious solution to the political problem was to substitute the Viper. The project was handed to Team Viper in February 1991, and they delivered a prototype for Carroll Shelby, who was fresh from a heart transplant. His mission was to give rides around the Speedway oval, to journalists and various VIPs. He was energetic, excited to be there, and clearly loved the car. It was a hot, beefy-red RT/10—no top. It was smooth and steady on the banked oval, and its V-10 produced a rumble as never heard from an American car. There were long lines for rides, and Shelby stayed til the last. He drove uncounted laps with blessed passengers at 130 miles an hour, his face beaming and his hair blowing in the wind as he bragged about the car.

Left

As the Viper was rushed through development for introduction in 1992, Team Viper quickly built a prototype to be used as the pace car at the 1991 Indy 500. Shelby drove the car for 1,800 trouble-free miles, mostly at speeds of more than 130 miles per hour. This gave Team Viper a boost of confidence as it prepared to start building the cars.

Below

For the first few years of Viper production, the car relied on removable side curtains instead of roll-up windows. Combined with the collapsing soft-top panel, the original car's weather protection left owners hoping for sunny days. *John Lamm*

Chrysler decided that the official media launch would baptize the Viper into the family of American sports cars. "We wanted Viper to be a continuation of American sport car heritage," said Tom Kowaleski, head of public relations at the time. We said, 'This is another part of American sports car history.' We did a great Friday night party at Phil Hill's place with American racers like Augie Pabst, Parnelli Jones, Sam Posey, Dan Gurney, and Carroll Shelby. Jay Leno was there too. We had one hell of a party. We also brought significant American race cars, so we had a Cobra, a Scarab, and *Ol' Yeller*. It was a great celebratory evening. That positioning really brought the car alive."

Auto scribes finally got to drive the car on the street the next day, followed by a day on the track. "We went up to the Las Padres Forest," Kowaleski said. "For people who wondered where you'd exercise a car like that in Southern California, boy, that was the place. Then we went to Willow Springs and raced the cars around the track the next day. We had fewer incidents, bent fenders, and whatever, than with anything else. I think it was the awareness of the power and what it could do."

Said Daniel Charles Ross, "I'll never forget how extraordinarily wide I thought it was the first time I saw it. Both edge-to-edge, but also the footprint of the tires, the rubber footprint. We'd never seen a car like that before, obviously. They'd shown us some limited imagery in the roundtables."

"You go on a press trip for a new Ferrari and you expect it to be a wonderful car, a great experience. Ferrari. You expect that. But who would have ever thought that Dodge could conceive of a car of this kind that would be so extraordinary, so expensive—and worth the money? Nobody could conceive of that. Nobody could process the information.

"A V-10! Whoever heard of a V-10? All that horsepower. Those huge tires. It was almost a hormonal experience. I think we would have been happy to just to touch it, and sit in it, and know that it was coming.

"The first time we got to drive it, most people stalled it the first time, because you couldn't believe it had that much clutch and that much grip. People barely suspected its capabilities, both in terms of power and handling."

Chrysler rounded up some of the most memorable American sports cars for the Viper's press introduction. The intended message was that the Viper is the continuation of the line begun by the likes of the Ford GT-40 and Shelby Cobra. *John Lamm*

Later, journalists drove it at the Chelsea Proving Grounds on a tight course laid out with pylons. "Nobody wanted to hurt it," said Ross. "You had two categories of drivers. You had the ones like me that would goose it a little in the corners to see what would happen. On the straights you had an opportunity to put your foot down, even though you almost didn't need to get out of first gear, and it was like being on a rocket sled. Literally, and for the first time for most, it was like nothing else we'd ever driven.

"Nobody ever got out if it without a big grin on their face. It was a formative experience, and extremely memorable."

The production RT/10 made its debut on schedule at the 1992 North American International Auto Show. But the rushed development prevented Team Viper from getting the engine where they wanted it on the first try. For example, the original RT/10 heads had hot spots in them, forcing Dodge to run a low 9.1:1 compression ratio, instead of the 10:1 compression ratio that was planned.

Addressing its flaws and compromises, Sjoberg explained, "To get the roadster out in 33 months, there was a cutoff. There was a time when you would have liked to have done more, and maybe saved some money and saved some weight, but there was a cutoff where there were no more changes unless it was safety or customer acceptance or a no-build kind of thing.

"We had an inventory of things we knew we wanted to do, that we knew [we] could do, and they were directionally right, but we were out of time. As we got along, the effort to launch the vehicle and make the changes we needed to make was reduced and we had more resources available, and we started to put more people on the project. And it turned out we learned how to make a lighter-weight engine, higher horsepower, better cooling, lower cost for the coupe."

"I went on some of the early drives, down in Santa Fe," said veteran auto writer Bob Storck. "Roy was along, and on one occasion I can recall us flailing it on some back New Mexico roads. I always pull in my enthusiasm several notches when I'm driving with a corporate guy, but Roy was saying, 'What are you wussing it for? This thing can do it! Go in deeper!'

"He was showing no fear in the car. His enthusiasm was allowing him to trust my abilities perhaps more than he should. The Viper did everything we asked of it. We were driving the thing rather hard in some high temperatures with a little bit of altitude, and we did have a minor engine stutter.

"We pulled into this Mexican restaurant. Here's Roy Sjoberg and a couple of the engineers running diagnostic codes on the engine, calling back to Detroit with their cell phones, comparing symptoms and diagnostic codes. By the time we came out of the lunch, the problems were all resolved."

"I don't think I'd modify the design in any way," said Lutz. "I don't think I'd modify the chassis structure. If I had it to do again, I don't think that I'd use the side exhaust, because they just produced

Phil Hill, Jean Sage, Francois Castaing, and Carroll Shelby attend the Viper's press launch to share in the thrill of witnessing the birth of a new legend in the American sports car pantheon. *John Lamm*

While Bob Lutz was justifiably proud to unveil the Viper concept car at the 1989 North American International Auto Show, it was an even prouder moment when, at the 1992 edition of the show, he introduced the production car. *John Lamm*

a terrible sound. I really think that bringing the exhaust out the back, like we did first on the coupes, and now on all of them, really produces a better sound.

"It is a great question in my mind, now knowing all the problems we would encounter in the launch, if we had selected the plastic technology that we did. We just had an incredibly tough time getting cars out. I don't know how it's going now; I hope they've finally got it down.

"The Viper I've got at home is number two," Lutz continued, "and that one was massaged and massaged and massaged until hell wouldn't have it, but it's still got a lot of flaws in the plastic. It is starting to develop sink marks in the hood and everything. I think it gives it character and legitimizes it as one of the early cars, but it would have cost us a little more to do it in metal and maybe we should have.

"There is no question about it, the car needed refinement. It needed a little bit more predictable handling, it needed less noise, it needed better body panel fit, it needed a nicer instrument panel. There's no sense asking a customer to give up slickness and refinement just because he has terrific performance. For roughly $70,000, he should get it all."

Said Tom Gale, "There are always things that you would fix or change, especially given hindsight. But when you examine what we were trying to do and what we've done subsequently, in the beginning it was really back to basics. We had a mantra, and it was 'Back to basics.'

"We had to continue to discipline ourselves not to let it go too far. Because we probably couldn't have delivered on the expectation and we might have compromised the very things that made it, in retrospect, so important. Performance was certainly the number one attribute we wouldn't compromise. And yet we had to meet all of the requirements that were in front of us, in terms of the law.

"We didn't want to be like anyone else. We didn't want to make those compromises. So it ended up having a top that was just applied, it ended up having a lot of horsepower, and a much different proportion and a far different capability than anyone else's vehicle.

"You could call it crude, you could call it whatever you wanted to. But it was badass. It got the job done. When you lined up at the light next to anyone else's sports car, it didn't matter whose, they were fiddling with the radio and they didn't want to know you were there. That was just part of the car.

"It is still to this day true, but we have been able to make a lot of refinements, and as we go forward you'll see it happen even more so. At the time we didn't have the capability to deliver on much more. We didn't have the ability with the small team and with the kind of ragtag way we had to do it. I'm glad we did it that way. For the time, it was the right thing to do.

"There isn't a lot I would change. Would you make this bigger or that bigger or this more robust? Yeah, sure, there are all kinds of things you might do that way. But all in all, when you look at the tradeoffs, when you look at the things we had to do without making serious compromises . . ."

Gale didn't finish the self-rating, but he didn't need to. Imperfect though it was, the Viper was quite an accomplishment. Especially, as he pointed out, "At first, nobody wanted to hear about it because everybody was up to their whatever in alligators."

The sensational early visceral Vipers were a work in progress. Team Viper heard the criticisms of the 1992 RT/10 and bit their tongues. The GTS Coupe would fix all that. The concept of the coupe was scheduled to appear at the 1993 Detroit show.

CHAPTER FOUR

RT/10 ROADSTER

The Viper's stunning styling might cause one to think that's what the car is all about, but the Viper is all about engine. The aluminum V-10 is the car's enormous centerpiece. It displaces 8.0 liters, or a whopping 488 cubic inches (and it'll be 8.3 liters in the 2003 Viper). When it's rumbling, it dominates the car and everything in it. The driver and passenger feel like they're riding an engine with wheels. Even when the engine is silent, its presence is inescapable. Besides filling the front of the car, it dictates the rest of it. The transmission, brakes, wheels, and tires are all massive in order to handle the onslaught of power. Even the unconventional windshield wipers are a result of the size of the engine. There was no space for a conventional wiper motor, so each blade gets its own small motor.

The frustrating relationship with Lamborghini aside, the bare engine block is a work of art. There is an Italian influence. Its massively deep-skirted design, with six-bolt main bearings, seems intended for racing. The block is unique in having an external water manifold to carry coolant to each cylinder individually. The thermostat was originally mounted at the back of the engine, so coolant hoses snaked over the engine to the radiator. The head casting was designed to provide a good swirl of the intake charge for efficient combustion to reduce emissions. At the bottom end, the Viper engine substituted a forged crankshaft with enlarged bearing journals for durability.

The weight-saving aluminum construction whacked 100 pounds off the original engine's weight compared to the cast-iron truck engine. But the engine weighed a still-hefty 716 pounds; 80 pounds more were trimmed for the 1996 GTS Coupe.

The year 1996 marked the arrival of the red-and-yellow "ketchup-and-mustard" paint scheme, complete with Ferrari-like yellow shields on the fenders.

The Viper's engine mounts the accessories, such as the alternator and air conditioning compressor, directly to the timing chain cover and drives them with a serpentine belt, helping save space in the engine bay.

Another unglamorous casting, the oil pan, also features some clever design ideas. Where most engines employ a bolt-on pick-up pipe for the oil pump to suck oil out of the sump in the oil pan, the Viper's oil pan is cast with an integral oil passage that picks up from the bottom of the pan. This lets the pan be shallower and lets the pickup use all of the oil in the sump. Conventional pick-ups leave some oil in the bottom of the sump. A bolt-on baffle in the pan shepherds the oil toward the pick-up, so that it doesn't suck air during hard cornering at the racetrack.

The radiator might not seem like an area ripe for innovation, but the Viper uses a special design that improves heat dissipation without enlarging the coolant volume or increasing the surface area of

"Red Intake Plenum and Valve Covers" may lack the lyrical sound of Ferrari's Testarossa "redhead" moniker, though the Viper's engine displays plenty of red paint. Regardless, the color is probably the least memorable of the V-10's qualities. *John Lamm*

The Viper RT/10 Roadster began life in 1992 with fabricated steel suspension arms and cast-iron hub carriers. But in 1996 the roadster received the cast-aluminum suspension parts shown here, taking 60 pounds off the car's unsprung weight. The new parts also employed different geometry aimed at making the Viper more stable.

The Viper's six-speed transmission was designed by Borg-Warner and is now supplied by Transmission Technologies Corporation. The transmission was under development for General Motors for the Camaro/Firebird when Chrysler signed on, striking a co-op deal with Corvette. *Transmission Technologies Corporation.*

the radiator. Instead, the inside of the coolant tubes in the double-row radiator are "turbulated." That means that they are dimpled, like the surface of a golf ball, to increase heat transfer from the water to the cooling fins.

Without the dimples to induce turbulence in the flowing water, a boundary layer of cooler water clings to the inner walls of the tubes, insulating the hotter water from transferring its heat to the fins. The same phenomenon makes bath water feel cool until the bather stirs it, breaking the cool boundary layer with turbulence. The system adds no weight, but increases the Viper's cooling capacity.

Another unusual detail is the water separator in the intake system. The NACA duct on the leading edge of the hood since the introduction of the GTS Coupe provides cold air directly into the engine's air cleaner. But the scoop can ingest water as well as air, and engines tend not to like breathing water. The solution is a bit like the design of baffles in a muffler.

The incoming air swirls around the baffles relatively easily, while the water, like sound waves in a muffler, strikes the baffles. After striking these transverse vanes in the air box, the water runs down to collect in the bottom. The trough is drained by a trio of "duck-bill" valves that open from the weight of the water releasing it, but remain closed the rest of the time to prevent air from entering.

The engine empties its exhaust through tubular headers into an exhaust system that has been a prominent aspect of the car. Initially, the Viper RT/10 employed side pipes, in obvious homage to the Cobra's 1960s-style layout. The concept car and early prototypes were even more radical, with exposed header pipes at the trailing edge of the front fenders.

That didn't make it to production for obvious reasons, but Chrysler was able to cram mufflers and catalysts into the truncated side-pipe system for the 1992–1995 RT/10. Routing the pipes, and especially the blisteringly hot catalysts (which operate at temperatures of 1,000 degrees Fahrenheit) in the doorsills, meant occupants would be exposed to excessive heat. So the company dug up some racing technology to insulate the sills from the heat. Racers employ Nomex to prevent burns from fires, but the aerospace industry uses it in pressed spaceboard form as an insulator. Dodge's designers

The year 1996 was one of significant changes for the Viper RT/10 Roadster. The car got even faster, with engine horsepower bumped up to 415, letting drivers blur the scenery even more easily.

By 1993, Team Viper had a chance to mix up some new paint options, such as this breathtaking black. Other colors available in 1994 included emerald green and bright yellow. A black-and-tan interior also became an option.

slipped in a sandwich of two 3-millimeter layers of Nomex to shield the outer sill from the blast furnace of heat only inches away. Another sheet of aluminum foil lines the floorpan to reflect heat that might otherwise melt the carpeting.

New EPA emissions requirements for 1996 mandated use of an oxygen sensor after the catalysts, and Chrysler's supplier didn't have one that could withstand both the extreme temperatures of the short exhaust system and the water it would be exposed to when driving in the rain.

Team Viper's solution was to switch to a rear exhaust that would permit free-flowing mufflers for better performance, while meeting the EPA's On Board Diagnostic II regulations. Viper owners may have preferred the side pipes, but few would complain about a power increase.

Routing the exhaust out the back, through a single muffler under the trunk floor, gave the Viper a lower-pitched sound that many found preferable to the side-pipe–equipped models. But it meant that the blast of heat would be carried to new parts of the car, so the Viper's tail needed some heat shielding too. The solution was an insulated aluminum panel that deflects the heat from the plastic gas tank and the trunk floor, preventing a repeat of the melted gas tank that occurred during tire testing of an early coupe prototype.

Because the catalysts still mount under the doorsills, those sills continue to be hot. The 2003 Viper returns to the original vision of side pipes thanks to the miracle of modern technology. The car uses a previously unavailable oxygen sensor that is both heat- and water-resistant, and new electronic noise-canceling mufflers that don't impose a horsepower penalty while meeting EPA noise requirements with the short exhaust pipes.

The T-56 six-speed gearbox is the product of a collaboration between Borg-Warner and Chrysler. Chrysler is called DaimlerChrysler these days, and Borg-Warner sold the T-56 to Tremec, so there have been some changes in the relationship, but the transmission remains essentially the same.

In addition to the hard-to-miss red-and-yellow combination, the 1996 model year also saw the introduction of white with blue stripes and black with silver stripes as optional color schemes for the RT/10 Roadster.

The horsepower increase in the 1996 Viper roadster was partly the result of a lower-restriction, rear-exiting exhaust system installed due to tightening emissions regulations. The change meant the temporary end of the beloved side pipes, until the arrival of the 2003 Viper.

Functionally, the Viper's T-56 is a close-ratio five-speed gearbox, with an absurdly tall sixth gear to help minimize the EPA gas-guzzler penalty on the car. The coupe is rated at an unlikely 21 miles per gallon highway, compared to a realistic 12 miles per gallon in the city.

The highway rating benefits from the torquey engine's ability to pull the impossibly tall gas miser gear, as well as a "skip shift" feature that nudges the shifter into the fourth-gear gate instead of second gear, when upshifting from first at part throttle. Worry not, dragstrip runs are unaffected, and even when the skip ship activates, a determined 1–2 upshift will still reach its intended destination rather than landing in fourth gear.

The Viper's ratios are 2.66:1 for first gear, 1.78:1 for second, and 1.30:1 in third. So far, so good. But fourth gear is a direct 1:1 ratio, more typical of fourth gear in a five-speed gearbox. Fifth is a .74:1 overdrive, as is typical for most cars, but the Viper still has another gear in its inventory; a .501:1 sixth that spins the output shaft at twice the engine's speed. The 490-foot-pound engine doesn't seem to mind, though it does seem in danger of falling asleep at legal highway speeds.

Viper owners are a dedicated lot, but they still don't like to get wet. Rain leaked around the original soft-roof panel, so for 1996 Dodge added an optional hard panel that reduced cockpit noise and helped plug the leaks.

The Viper features 13.0-inch vented disk brakes at all four corners, with aluminum calipers for light weight. The front calipers have four 42-millimeter pistons, while the rears use 38-millimeter single-piston calipers. But the Viper didn't stop as well as high-performance cars equipped with ABS.

Some Viper owners preferred their car without ABS, thinking that computer-controlled braking was antithetical to the Viper's philosophy. But the car routinely finished last in the braking category of magazine supercar comparisons, which was not good for proud Viper owners. When building the Viper, the primary performance target was to have the world's best 0-100-0-mile-per-hour performance, but the car was losing that test too. The brakes weren't holding up their side of the equation.

The solution was ABS, which would be installed on 2001 Vipers.

The Viper's body is just as unique as the hardware it covers. Most cars use steel bodywork. Some, such as the Saturn, use plastic, and the Corvette is famous for its use of fiberglass. Team Viper eschewed steel body panels for the same reasons it avoided a stamped-steel floorpan: tooling costs. In a low-budget, low-volume model such as the Viper, costly but durable steel stamping dies wouldn't be cost-effective.

Instead, the Viper would use plastic. This would give the team the ability to fiddle with design changes during development and to do things such as add an NACA duct and fender louvers in the 1996 and newer models. But it wouldn't be just any kind of plastic. Chrysler wanted to develop a new variety that is really more a combination of plastic and fiberglass.

Hot colors on the steering wheel, shift knob, and hand brake handle highlighted a previously dark interior.

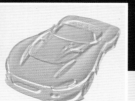

VIPER AFTERMARKET

In exchange for their loyalty, Viper owners want a company to be responsive to their needs and desires. Team Viper has held up its end of that bargain. Said Viper Owners Club of America president Tony Estes, "What we've asked for, and they've given us, is more power and better handling. My first Viper was 400 horsepower, and I said, 'Wow!' Then the second one was 450, and I said, 'Wow!' and had maybe a little bit of fear that this is more than I can handle. Then it becomes mundane, so you make some small modifications. That's the nice thing about the Viper. You can make some small modifications, without going into the motor, and add 50 to 60 rear-wheel horsepower."

The thriving aftermarket for Viper parts is an entire cottage industry. One might think that the Viper is underpowered, judging from the wide availability of hop-up parts for the engine.

"We put K&N filters in and gained 20 horsepower at the rear wheels," said Estes. "You're talking 25 horsepower at the crankshaft.

"With a light flywheel, they rev like a Kawasaki. Coming out of the corners it is unbelievable. They came out with an [engine management] computer that at Phoenix was good for a second-and-half a lap. All you do is take out the stock computer, put in the other one, and with the modifications, K&Ns, the header, they changed the fuel and timing curves, the car runs smoother, accelerates quicker.

"My race car has 15,000 miles on it and 13,000 of them are track miles. It has the original motor; the valve covers have never been off. The only thing we ever did was put K&N filters and headers on it, and it dynoed at 476 horsepower at the rear wheels. What more can you ask for? There are companies that will balance, blueprint, port, and polish, and you pick up a little bit, 30 to 40 horsepower."

Low-restriction air filters, custom headers, low-restriction exhaust systems, larger fuel-injection throttle bodies, custom heads and valvetrain, higher-performance cams, improved oil pans, bigger radiators and even turbochargers and superchargers are among the power-producing options available from a plethora of Viper accessory suppliers.

Despite the proliferation of power parts, more owners are recognizing the value of handling upgrades, so there are more suspension parts available now than in the past, Estes said. "Five years ago, everybody was trying to build more power. Then they realized the car didn't go any faster around the track with more power; they needed to tweak the handling a little bit. For the track you can always stiffen the springs and lower the car."

Viper owners can also choose from a wide variety of upgraded brake pads, or they can completely replace the large factory rotors and calipers with enormous racing units. For the Viper owner who lusts after the antilock brakes on the 2001 and newer cars, but who doesn't want to have to buy a new car, the same ABS system used on the Porsche 911 Turbo is available for $9,500. Pricey, but cheaper than buying a new car to get ABS.

Upgraded transmissions are available that will take the additional power of a modified engine, along with replacement torque biasing differentials that fit right into the factory housing and will help put power to the ground more effectively than the stock unit. Beefier halfshafts help the power reach the wheels without snapping off any drivetrain components.

In case Viper owners feel the car's styling is too mild, there are replacements for every removable panel on the car. New hoods, fascias, spoilers, wings, and anything else that might be attached to a sports car are available for the Viper, usually from multiple vendors.

DaimlerChrysler's in-house aftermarket company, Mopar Performance Parts, got in on the act with a bunch of Viper hot-rod parts labeled "for racing only." Complete engines are available for those unfortunates who have blown their engines, or who have to suffer with the paltry 400 horsepower of the early Viper engines. ■

The red-and-yellow scheme, complete with a yellow shield on the trailing edge of the front fenders, was a clear homage to famous old Ferrari racing cars, such as the 1958 Testa Rossa posing with the Viper. *John Lamm*

In the resin transfer mold (RTM) process, glass fibers are placed in a mold and, once the mold is closed, injected with resin, which mixes with the fiberglass to form the part. This differs from the more common sheet molded compound (SMC) process, where a glass mat that has already been impregnated with resin is stamped in a mold at high pressure. RTM produces stronger panels with easier-to-control finish quality than SMC. SMC, in contrast, is more labor-intensive and demands higher pressure in the molds.

The difference is that an RTM panel needs only 10 to 15 minutes of hand finishing to achieve "Class A" appearance, defined as an exposed surface finish that must be pleasing at all times. An SMC panel may require hours of work to reach the same level, according to Russell Spencer, who was the Viper technology development executive responsible for the bodywork.

"With any production run up to 20,000 units, RTM tooling will give you high-quality pieces," he said. It is also conducive to making changes along the way. "If product design came to us and said, 'We want to change the look of the Viper,' with RTM, we could accomplish it with a one-year lead time. You can't do that with regular steel tooling. With a niche vehicle like the Viper, you must be able to respond to quick changes in the marketplace, and we can," said Spencer.

The RTM body panels are lighter than metal panels by as much as 40 percent. European sports cars, such as the BMW Z1, Alfa Romeo SZ, Lotus Elan, and Lotus Esprit, have also used RTM plastic, but they used thicker, heavier plastic than the Viper.

"The difference is that those cars use RTM panels with a thickness of 1/8 inch or more," said Spencer. "We're working with thicknesses of no more than 1/10 of an inch," he said. "To do RTM

Five-spoke wheels replaced the original three-spoke design in 1996, updating the car's otherwise unchanged styling.

panels of that reduced thickness, suitable for 'Class A' exposure, represents quite an advance. We knew it would be risky, because finish is so important to the customer. However, we addressed that issue carefully, and I believe we succeeded."

The quality of parts being made is measured by a computer-controlled process call the "defraction technique." A light is flashed over the panel at a low angle and the reflections are photographed and analyzed for waviness that would indicate surface variations. This technique exaggerates any imperfections, making them easier to spot.

The target for perfection is a sheet of the finest plate glass, which would score a 0 on a scale of 0 to 1,000. To pass muster for the Viper, panels must rate a score of 150 or better. Nickel plating on the molds contributes to this high quality.

RTM is also applied innovatively in the Viper's windshield frame. The frame has a foam-wrapped steel center, with an RTM composite outer surface. This is not only lighter and smaller than a steel frame, its one-piece design extends into the dashboard, forming the top of the instrument panel. That means fewer parts are needed, making correct fit and finish easier.

Another unusual aspect of the Viper's windshield is the wipers. As any owner noticed the first time the wipers were switched on, they work, well, strangely. They aren't synchronized quite the same way most wipers are, and the driver's-side wiper runs through a full stroke before the passenger's-side

The new five-spoke wheels were body-color on the white Viper in 1996, giving the car a more understated monochrome appearance. *Understated* isn't a term that's often used with the Viper.

The year 1996 saw a new chassis and aluminum suspension components designed for the GTS Coupe. The chassis was lighter and stronger, thanks to increased use of alloys and changes to the frame's tubular structure.

For 1997, the RT/10 Roadster received the engine that was introduced in the 1996 GTS Coupe. It weighed less and boosted power to an even 450 from the previous year's 415 horses. Roll-up windows, another coupe innovation, also appeared on the roadster in 1997.

starts up. For a split second, it can seem that the passengers' side wiper arm has come loose. But then, right on schedule, it springs to life.

The reason for this odd performance is that the wipers are each controlled separately by their own motor. If the Viper is the "more is better" car, then maybe more wiper motors were appropriate. The real reason for the two-motor approach is unsurprising: the 8.0-liter V-10 is so big it leaves no space for a conventional wiper motor.

The problem was that most cars use a single, large wiper motor mounted in the middle of the firewall. But the engine was so large, there was no space for one. The solution is a pair of minivan rear wiper motors. Because the rear motors are mounted inside the vans, not underhood where they are exposed to the elements, they had to be weatherized for duty in a hostile environment.

They also had to be programmed to coordinate, because the wiper blades overlap and their strokes had to be coordinated. But those problems were more easily solved than violating the law of physics that dictates no two objects can occupy the same space at the same time, which would have been necessary to use the traditional wiper system.

The Viper's crash safety systems are state of the art and unfortunately have been tested by many owners. The good news is that they often attest to the car's tremendous safety in the event of a collision. The Viper's three-point belts work with the air bag system to provide occupant restraint in the event of a crash. The air bag module was the smallest available for the car's 14-inch steering wheel when Chrysler added the air bags to the Viper.

Despite an all-new chassis and engine that made the Viper lighter, stronger, faster, and better handling, the solid red roadster still looked the same as the 1992 car. The five-spoke wheels are a giveaway on this car.

During development of the second-generation chassis, tire supplier Michelin faced the challenge of building tires that suited the different characteristics of the prototype coupe and the roadster (inside garage). *Ken Payne*

Unlike most air bags, which have vents sewn in them for the hot gas inside to escape, the Viper's bags are made of woven nylon. It lets the gas escape through the surface of the bag, so it doesn't have a few superheated vents after deployment. Special interior exhaust vents in the fender area of the cargo compartment let air out of the interior without letting it in. This means that the pressure from an air bag deployment is quickly released from inside the car. It also means that it is easy to close the doors with the windows up, because pressure isn't trapped inside that makes it harder to close them.

A collapsible steering column prevents transfer of impact force through the steering column to the driver. GTS Coupe buyers who choose the ACR package are even better protected by the five-point racing harness included in those cars (although the street production-spec three-point belts are also included).

The Viper's doors were reinforced to meet the National Highway Traffic Safety Administration's requirements for side-impact protection. These later cars add 2-inch blocks of high-density foam to the intrusion protection beams already inside the doors. The foam helps spread the load of an impact over a larger area. On the coupes and second-generation roadsters, the door striker brackets, door hinge, and door-to-sill interlock were all reinforced, and the tops of the doors were strengthened to support the glass windows in the doors.

All of this attractive hardware needs some protection of its own, so the Viper includes an antitheft system designed to make it a little harder for unauthorized people to drive the car. The vehicle theft alarm (VTA) is integrated with the remote keyless entry system and is armed by locking the doors with the remote or with the door-lock switch.

It is disarmed by unlocking the doors with the remote. The VTA monitors the ignition switch, hood switch, door switches, and in the coupe, the hatch switch. Opening any of these areas, or attempting to start the car without first disarming the system triggers the horn for two and a half minutes and flashes the parking lights for up to 18 minutes. The fuel-injection system is also disabled, so the engine won't run until the system has been disarmed. A special steering wheel lock cylinder breaks internally if a thief yanks it out with a slide hammer, leaving the part intact that prevents the ignition from being turned on.

With luck, drivers will never need the protection systems for themselves or their Viper, so they can just enjoy the rest of the cool hardware Team Viper put in the car.

Michelin tire test engineer Ken Payne is at the wheel of a Viper coupe while technicians check tire temperatures and pressures following a test session at Road Atlanta. *Ken Payne*

Ken Payne, Michelin project manager for O.E. tire development, was test engineer, manager, and, ultimately, supervisor for the development of the Viper's tires. He remembers the company's effort to develop tires while Chrysler was still developing the car that would wear them:

"We formed a team within the Michelin organization to do development of the tires for the Viper. It started by taking the information they had relative to size and vehicle and performance characteristics and working with existing performance tire lines we had. Starting off, I did early testing on a Corvette we had as our basic mule, to get an idea what the tuning would be for the tire. Then once we had molds and tooling available to build actual Viper sizes, the process started there.

"We did a lot fundamental work, looking at wet performance and noise and general handling at our proving ground," Payne said. "Then, when it became an active tire development program at Team Viper on the Chrysler side, then we got into the process of giving them development tires, doing joint tests with them, getting prototypes here and there for testing either at Michelin or we would go off and test at their facilities.

"We did tons of testing at Road Atlanta and other tracks around the country. That became an iterative process. We'd use the term *submission*, where we'd submit tires. Typically, every couple of months we have a series of tires we'd submit. I worked extensively with Herb Helbig and Neil Hanneman and the hands-on vehicle development guys. Neil was my testing counterpart during that time frame.

"We tested in the original V-8 mule, which unfortunately at our first test session at Road Atlanta, broke the gearbox almost immediately. But that car—other than that it was completely ugly—was an absolute delight to drive because it had wonderful balance, because it was so light in the front end, and because it was the first. You always have fondness for those firsts.

"We went through the process, competitively at first, with Goodyear. Then there was what loosely got nicknamed the 'Halloween shootout.' All along, the Viper development team was trying to make this car a technical statement and a technically based project. That meant whoever was the right tire, in terms of their performance objectives, was going to get their business.

"It came down to a shootout, where they wanted to cut it down to one supplier, because the

Experience during wet tire testing showed the need for the plastic fender liners under the Viper's hood to keep road spray off the ignition system. *John Lamm*

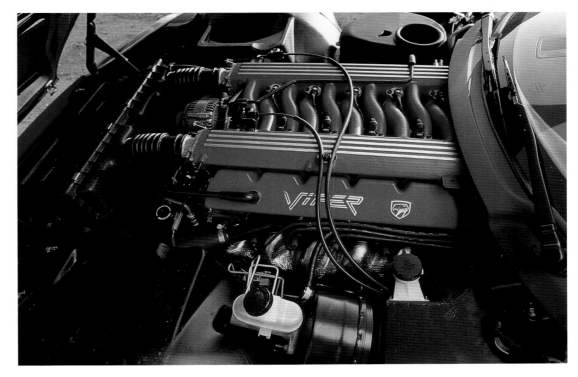

resources they had were limited and our resources were limited, so [we] didn't want to have to continue slogging in a competitive situation. So there was this shootout that was around Halloween. We had developed a really good rapport with the Viper team, so we sent them tires with pumpkins and things stuck on the side for entertainment.

"We ultimately won the technical battle. I think from the beginning we had a very good idea of the performance they wanted in terms of vehicle handling and balance, and we hit it very well with our early development tires. That put us in the right position at the right time to succeed in getting the car's business.

"Then we got into the real meat of development. Chris and I spent many weeks out in Arizona working during the winter months with Neil on vehicles. Typical with anything new like that in vehicle development, you have all sorts of interesting things develop. We might go out and have tires that perform as Chris expected and we might have tires that were like, 'Oooh, this combination isn't gonna work.'

"At the same time, the car was constantly evolving. We might go out and come back in to do a tire change and find the oil pan is cracked. They were doing prototype baffles and things like that. Or you'd come in from a run where you've been dogging the car really hard and find this generation of insulation around the side sill exhaust system isn't gonna work as fumes are coming up from the carpets that are melting in the car. Little flames occasionally erupting from things like that. It was multitudes of things happening. Doing hard launches, we would find that U-joint isn't up to the task when the driveshaft stops turning. That is all standard fare that goes on in development.

"It became immediately clear that the nature of the car was somewhat brutal, but in a wonderful sense. I envisioned this thing as being a modern-day Cobra or a Lotus Seven on steroids.

"The wet testing for the vehicle, they pretty much trusted us to set what we felt were the right levels of performance for the market at that time. So we would take the appropriate cars and tires to benchmark it against. At the time the ZR-1 was a new bogey on the radar screen, so that was one of the levels of performance.

"They shipped prototypes to the track for me to use in our wet testing facility. The first car they sent had no top, of course, because Vipers aren't really supposed to have a top. It had no windows and it had no windshield wipers, but that [was] just a minor inconvenience. I just donned a helmet and put on a rainsuit and went out and got wet.

The warning sticker in the doorjamb points to the doorsill as a reminder that the blistering-hot exhaust pipes and catalytic converters are only inches away. *John Lamm*

"We use sprinklers to wet the track mounted in boxes below pavement surface, and they shoot through slots in the tops of the boxes. So you are constantly driving through a rainstorm.

"We were helping them develop the vehicles in some areas. The first vehicle had no inner fender liners. Half a lap into my first trip around our lateral adherence circle, the car stopped. There was no water protection for the engine management box that was mounted in the engine bay and the water coming up off the wheels was dousing it and just shut everything down.

"So we dragged it off the circle, quickly field-fabbed a Plexiglas cover for it, and we were back in business. That sort of stuff was fun. From my days of driving TR-3s in college in the rain with no top, I was right at home with that.

"For a typical tire development session, Chrysler would bring the current-level car. Typically Neil Hanneman and Herb Helbig and some of the other Team Viper guys would come. And we'd have a matrix of tires, maybe eight different constructions of rear tires and some number of different constructions of front tires. We start with a reference set, either that is the preferred tire from a previous session, or some other tire we have mutually agreed on as our baseline to start with. Both Neil and I would go out and drive our tires and get dialed in as to the feel of them.

"We used a rating scale almost like Olympic scoring, a 10-point scale. Then we'd have a bunch of criteria that we'd evaluate the performance on. Things like initial turn-in response, the precision through the corner, how well it follows the path once you've placed it onto the line through the corner, the lateral firmness of the tire—what does it feel like when you turn in? Does it feel planted, or does it feel like it is moving laterally across the contact patch? Many different criteria like that.

"We'd establish a nominal value of a 7.0 on a reference tire, and each other construction in that matrix of tires; each of us would test them and rate that tire for all these different criteria against that reference tire. If it's better it gets a higher score. You might say this tire is better for initial turn-in so it might get an 8 for the initial turn-in. But on corner exit, it might have had too much understeer, so there it would drop below the reference, say, with a 6.0.

"We do that for all those criteria on one set of tires. You go to the next combination; you do the same thing. And you just sequence through all the different tire combinations for that test, with regular reruns of the reference tire to make sure you are calibrated still on what that reference level was.

"Throughout this it is an absolute necessity to be driving the car near its potential, because that was the emphasis of Viper: We're going to run this car hard and we want maximum potential out of it. But you always had to be fair to every set of tires. You had to be repeatable in how you were using the car. You also—because these were prototypes and constantly under development and often early on we were developing pieces of the car at the same time—you had to make the car live. You had to be able to drive very quickly, very thoroughly evaluate the performance, but also be very friendly to the machinery.

"I equate it much like endurance racing. You have to extract the maximum potential out of the vehicle, without using up the vehicle. That was critical. If it meant shifting it at 5,000 rpm, instead of banging it to redline every time through the gears, that's what you did. Ultimately, it doesn't have much of an impact on the lap times that you are turning."

CHAPTER FIVE

THE COUPE

The coupe arrived wearing the blue-with-white-stripes livery of the famous Cobra Daytona Coupe, which provided inspiration for the car. Daytona designer Peter Brock said that the paint scheme was the link, but after that the Viper is an original—including the styling. *John Lamm*

When the Dodge Viper came to the market in 1992, in terms of its detail and refinement, it was not much more than a factory-engineered, government-approved kit car. It had imposing styling and a unique engine, but its roughness around the edges made it apparent that corners had been cut. What never is apparent, though, are the reasons: budget and schedule. Not enough money, not enough time.

Tom Gale started working on the GTS while the roadster was being built. In the spirit of the original Viper, he worked almost covertly, without going through channels, and hid the design costs.

"It was fairly clear we really did need something else," he said. "But there wasn't much corporate interest. People asked, 'Who are you going to sell these to?'

"You are going to sell one to everyone who bought a roadster. These people are out there."

Team Viper badly wanted to build a follow-up car for many reasons, not least of which was getting it right. And they were ambitious.

"Our goal was to create one of the world's premiere grand touring cars," said Gale. "The roadster was designed for the aggressive, wind-in-the-hair driver. The GTS Coupe had the same capacity but in a more refined manner."

Gale believed that while people could tolerate the roadster's shortcomings to enjoy its stunning performance, most of them would rather be comfortable while doing it. An upgraded Viper would make the car more appealing, he argued—eventually, successfully. "The redesign gave it windows, it gave it air conditioning, it gave it weather protection, so you could drive the car in a much different environment. It also stiffened it up; it did a lot of things for it functionally."

"I really looked forward to the coupe," said Bob Storck. "That was the point where the Viper really started the refinement. Not only things like the roll-up windows, but the chassis and suspension gained big improvements. They were able to take the time to study and to tweak and make the thing work."

Gale built the concept coupe in the same quiet shop 8 miles down the road from headquarters, the same shop where the roadster had taken shape in clay, under cover. Said Gale, "That car belonged to the design office. At the time, all of the concept cars were done for the administrative side of the house or for the marketing side of the house. That one always belonged to the design office because I had to do it and hide it under my own budget."

The now-trademark blue-and-white paint scheme was planned to help establish a characteristic appearance for the coupe, much as the "classic" roadster was solid red with three-spoke wheels. "We wanted to paint it blue with the white stripes," said Gale. "We wanted to carve out the territory, that that graphic kind of belonged to us. We protected it all along and it has become an important part of Viper. It has become an important device. That was the kind of turf you stake out when you do those things."

"We built a pickup truck, a new Ram, to haul it," said Gale. "We built a blue-and-white Viper-engined Ram, painted the trailer that had the Viper on it. That was all part of the package for that particular car."

At the Detroit show, the Viper GTS Coupe concept car was displayed on a custom trailer, hitched to a matching Dodge Ram pickup with a Viper engine. It was as big a hit as the RT/10 had been four

The Viper GTS Coupe was a redesigned car under the skin, as more than 90 percent of the car was new. Even with a fixed roof and large glass rear hatch adding weight, the coupe was lighter than the original roadster.

An all-new frame shed 60 pounds but was 25 percent stiffer in torsional rigidity, thanks to computer analysis that revealed where the frame needed to be strengthened and where it carried extra weight that didn't contribute to stiffness.

The 1996 coupe replaced these fabricated steel suspension arms and heavy iron steering knuckles with elegant cast-aluminum parts that slashed unsprung weight by 60 pounds.

years earlier. Fortunately, Team Viper had been gearing up for production. Now the team had to start planning how to build the car.

It all fell to Roy Sjoberg and his people. "We started out with the roadster, and the purpose was to minimize the resources and minimize the up-front investment of $50 million and 50 people," he said. "With that budget you can't do multiple vehicles. We built one design and built one car. Period. That was a roadster with only one color and only one interior, and initially we weren't even going to have air conditioning, but that became an absolute must for the customers. But always, the background was to have a coupe that was more user-friendly.

"We had learned some things. When you've never done it before, you design with a little excess, a safety factor to meet the crash tests. Now we had a car, we'd hit enough barriers, we knew how well it performed and we knew what we could change and not have an impact on performance and yet have a significant impact on weight. It was about a 140-pound reduction in the coupe. We added a roof, which was more weight, so we ended up with a vehicle that had more content but was slightly lighter than the original roadster."

The design compromises made in rushing the RT/10 were addressed by the coupe. And the improvements in the coupe were transferred into the new roadsters, which got the coupe's chassis upgrades in 1996 and its new engine the following year.

The GTS Coupe included a wide array of improvements, aimed at lightening the car, making it more powerful, easier to drive, and more refined. Some of the changes were obvious but probably not terribly important. Door releases on the outside and power-operated, roll-down glass windows are improvements that helped distinguish the Viper from mere kit cars, such as the clones of Shelby's original Cobra.

The roadster body didn't change at all, and the coupe's only outward difference was the fixed roof. But Team Viper basically jacked up that unchanged body and rolled a new car into place underneath.

"They literally redid the car," said Shelby Cobra Daytona Coupe designer Peter Brock. "When they really realized there was a market out there, after doing the RT/10, they sat down and redesigned the car as a coupe. It was like a 98 percent new car when they finished with it. It just upgraded so terrifically from the roadster."

Brock exaggerates only by 8 percent. In fact, more than 90 percent of the Viper's parts were changed for the GTS Coupe.

Under the hood, which is where the interest of most Viper enthusiasts lies, the new engine was 80 pounds lighter and had 35 more horsepower, giving it an eye-bulging 440. It featured an impressive redesigned cooling system, efficient and stable, holding cylinder variation to a remarkable 3 degrees Fahrenheit. One problem with the original engine's design was marginal cooling, especially of the cylinder heads. Because of problems with hot spots in the heads, Dodge had to back off to a 9:1 compression ratio, from the desired 10:1, to eliminate detonation.

There was also a new frame, 60 pounds lighter with 25 percent better torsional rigidity and 12 percent better beam strength. New computer technology enabled them to analyze the efficiency of the RT/10 tube structure, and, said Roy Sjoberg, "It turned out we could lighten the frame." So the GTS got optimized tube sizes—in diameter and wall thickness—and stiffened joints. Mounts for the differential were reinforced to increase stability of the housing under hard acceleration.

With a lighter engine in front and a large glass hatch in the back, the GTS Coupe's weight distribution shifted rearward, so the shocks and springs were new. To make the car friendlier during

This gorgeous prototype looks like a production GTS Coupe but differs in a few details. The car features dummy side pipes, despite the use of the rear exhaust on the coupe, and the center brake light is a plain horizontal bar, while the brake light on production cars is integrated into the Viper icon.

aggressive driving, a bit of understeer was dialed in. The RT/10's steel control arms (also known as A-arms or wishbones) and cast-iron hub carriers (also known as steering knuckles or uprights) were replaced with cast-aluminum units that slashed a whopping 60 pounds from the car's unspring weight, which is weight not suspended by the springs. Less unsprung weight allows the suspension to better follow the contours of the road.

The reduced unsprung weight led to changes in the valving of the shocks, giving drivers a better ride to go with the better handling. The American Club Racing package–equipped GTS Coupes feature adjustable shocks with external fluid reservoirs for maximum performance under extreme conditions.

The rear suspension geometry was revised for more stable handling. The mounts were shifted to lower the roll center and reduce bump steer. The rear caster angle (the angle the rear hub carrier is tilted fore and aft) was changed from -6 degrees to +1 degree, for improved straight-line stability.

The front geometry was not changed, but the lower ball joint was moved from the hub carrier to the control arm for more stiffness under braking. The shock mounts were relocated farther outboard on the front control arms for increased shock travel. The suspension travel was unchanged, but for the same amount of wheel travel the shocks now travel farther through their stroke, which gives them a better chance to control the movement precisely.

The coupe's dramatic styling, especially when finished in the signature Viper Blue with white stripes, was a clear homage to Peter Brock's Daytona, although there are other influences in the car's design. But said Brock, "I think the GTS will stand alone as its own icon. People see a lot of similarities now, but as time goes on, I think the car will begin to stand on its own, much as the

Despite the same paint job, no one mistook the Dodge Ram VTS concept truck for a Cobra Daytona Coupe. As part of the introduction of the GTS Coupe concept car, Dodge rolled the new Viper out on a trailer pulled by this specially painted Ram truck. The paint job inspired some Viper owners to paint their Rams in similar fashion.

The plan was for the Viper to follow the matching Ram on a trailer. Apparently the Viper prefers to lead. *John Lamm*

Daytona stands on its own and the GTO stands on its own today. But we won't really know that for another 10, maybe 15, years. Time really tells you what the icons of each period are. I think the Viper coupe will turn out to be one of those great designs from this period.

"In truth, the car was not a copy or a take-off on the Daytona," Brock continued. "It was a combination of several cars from that period. The look really came from the paint scheme. That was the American car, but there are some things that are as much Ferrari GTO as it was Daytona.

"There's no question that Chrysler's marketing people used the color scheme to emulate the Daytona. But Tom Gale was nice enough to contact me a year before they did that and show me the drawings and what their marketing plans were. He said that they planned to do a remake of the Daytona look with the stripes and everything, and he was nice enough to ask if it would be all right with me. I was honored by them even asking.

"They were so poor and had so little support from management when they first started the Viper project. This little enthusiast band of guys, they couldn't have gone from zero to the coupe first. They had to go through that interim stage to get approval. Once Chrysler found out there were people out there who were willing to go with it, then they were bold enough to go ahead and redo the car and make it into what it was.

"The coupe really was a design of its own. I don't think in any way that it was a copy. I think they did something very nicely on their own, without any real inspiration from the Daytona."

The mighty V-10 engine sits behind the Viper's front wheel centerline, shifting some of its weight to the rear for better handling. The clamshell hood, however, limits access to the engine bay. It is being replaced by a conventional hood and fenders on the 2003 Viper.

The V-10 had to fit under the Viper's low hood, posing a packaging challenge for designers. Thanks to a shallow, cast-aluminum oil pan and flattened intake runners at the top of the engine, the Viper's engine has the lowest height of any DaimlerChrysler 90 degree "vee" engine ever. It measures only 25.9 inches from top to bottom.

While it is still no match for a Mississippi River stern-wheeler, the Viper coupe's new engine boosted the car's power output to 450 horsepower and 490 foot-pounds of torque. Both machines have dual exhaust pipes.

The public got the message and saw the Cobra influence. "One of the things that was most gratifying to me was when we were doing the long lead introduction for journalists in Los Angeles, I had done my pitch and we were down on the street going through the cars before going for the ride," Gale recalled.

"Along came a passerby and he said, 'Wow, that looks just like a Cobra.' I thought, 'How gratifying.' It was really neat because he got it immediately, even though there wasn't a surface on the car that was even close, or remotely like, a Cobra. That is really what we were all about trying to do. If you fast-forward, that's what we were trying to do with [the P. T.] Cruiser too. It evokes images, it evokes memories, it elicits certain expressions without being literal."

Added Gale, "For the original clay model, if I could put two pictures on the wall that were the image icons, it was the Cobra Daytona Coupe and the Ferrari 250 GTO. If you look at the windshield,

Dodge upgraded the Viper's interior for the GTS Coupe, adding a new steering wheel with a magnesium rim and adjustable pedals.

By 1997, the roadster had received the coupe's new engine and chassis. So this race to Key Biscayne would likely have been a dead heat.

the way the roof is placed on the body, you can see some of each. The first model we did was red. I think you could see some of each. The way the tail ends, you can certainly see some of the Daytona Coupe. Certainly the color was inspired by the Daytona Coupe.

"You can see the influences in there. At least I can. But it's not one of those things where the first person who walks by is going to say, 'Wow, it looks like a GTO.' We really didn't want that."

Dodge stylists were able to approach the creation of a coupe the same way Shelby's team had years earlier. "The inspiration was very easy to carry over from the roadster, just as Shelby had done it, to take the roadster theme into the coupe," said John Herlitz. "And to do the very clever thing, that I think was so neat on the car, was the double-bubble roof cross section that gives a little more headroom.

"It was a fairly easy translation to do. A fellow by the name of Bob Hubbach was the designer of the coupe.

The coupe and roadster have swapped clothes in this shot, with the roadster painted in the coupe's racing stripes and the coupe wearing the roadster's solid red. The stripes make the coupe look longer and leaner.

Hubbach and Brock are good friends, so that worked out real well. It just so happened that Hubbach and Brock graduated from Art Center in the same class, or close to it."

"The design changes evolved as we had people and had the experiences," said Roy Sjoberg. "Then we just spun our race thoughts into the coupe. We thought that was a better vehicle to race because with the roof it had better aerodynamics. And we'd learned about some tricks we could do and have less cooling openings and more cooling for brakes and things like that. So it was the natural package to evolve into the racing vehicle."

The second-generation engine was also designed to go racing. When the new engine was developed, very precise cylinder-head casting techniques were employed that allowed the head to be lighter, with thinner water jackets for better heat transfer. The cooling passages were moved closer to hot spots such as the spark plug and exhaust valves to help carry heat away more efficiently. A smaller water volume in each head contributes to faster warm-up for lower cold-start exhaust emissions. Coolant, which flowed opposite the usual direction in the original Viper engine, now flowed more conventionally, and the thermostat was relocated to the front of the engine. The better cooling allowed the compression to be bumped up half a point, contributing to the power increase.

The all-important intake and exhaust ports were also reworked in the new heads for better power, efficiency, and emissions. The head bolts were shortened to trim 4.5 pounds in weight from the engine.

The new thin-wall-casting cylinder block lightened the Viper's burden by 20 pounds. More conventional dry pressed-in-iron cylinder liners replaced the heavier and labor-intensive wet liners. An example of better living through computers, a finite element analysis of the block showed

WALKAROUND

The GTS Coupe's body is entirely different from the roadster, although the body panels look nearly the same. In addition to the NACA intake duct in the center of the hood, the GTS Coupe has louvers in the front fenders that exhaust hot air from under the hood.

At the front, an extended lip protrudes below the grille. It serves the same purpose as a "splitter" on the race Vipers: it prevents air going into the grille from spilling over and going under the car. More air under the car means lift instead of downforce, which makes cars unstable at high speed.

The roof is an obvious addition, but it is slightly unconventional in cross-section, with a bubble over each seat for headroom. These are known as "Gurney blisters," after a story about Dan Gurney hammering out additional headroom in a race car he once drove. Now there is room for the occupants to wear helmets, which is a reasonable likelihood. A taller windshield also contributes to the roof's height.

The spacious interior also provides

A unique aspect of the GTS Coupe is the double-bubble roofline. The twin peaks provide plenty of headroom inside the car, leading to the belief that they were meant to provide the headroom needed for drivers wearing a helmet. It was a suggestion of the car's racing ambitions from day one.

enough room in the hatch area to hold a spare mammoth rear wheel and tire. The 20 cubic feet of space represents a 70 percent increase over the cargo space in the roadster's Spartan trunk.

The coupe's fuel filler was moved to the passenger-side B-pillar. There is a beautiful retro aluminum racing-style quick-release gas cap, which makes it look like the car should include a 10-gallon dump can for refueling. The cap is functional, but only leads to the screw-on plastic cap underneath. The tank holds 19 gallons, shrunk from 22 in order to gain cargo space.

The door hinges are aluminum, lighter and 1 inch thicker, stronger, and more stable. And the big news was exterior release switches. They are switches, rather than door handles, because the Viper has electronic switches that activate electric servo motors to release the door. Locks are also electrical, controlled by the key fob remote from outside the car or by switches mounted on the inner door panel inside the car.

The coupe's doors have glass windows inside them, unlike the original roadster's side-curtain design. Window switches on the center console control the electrically powered windows. Power windows may seem like an unnecessarily heavy luxury item on a bare-bones sports car, but the cockpit lacked the space for window cranks. Because the original roadster leaked so heavily, which was inevitable given its design, the builders of the coupe wanted to make the GTS perfect. Tubular rubber weather-stripping surrounds the door frame. The upper part has a lip for the window to seat against, and a clip on the window frame holds the glass in place at high speeds.

The headlights, fog lights, and center brake lamp are new. The headlights use special Halogen Infrared Reflective bulbs that reflect heat back into the filament, making it hotter and brighter than standard lamps. The fog lights have a revised pattern that is shallower and wider than the pattern of the earlier fog lights. The center brake light is an LED lamp instead of incandescent, as on the roadster. LED's light is faster, draws much less power, and never burns out.

The Coupe's seats are 20 pounds lighter and have increased travel fore and aft. The adjustable pedal mechanism, called a pedal sled, adds only 2 pounds. A magnesium-core steering wheel also contributes to weight savings.

On the dashboard, the tach and speedometer were moved into side-by-side positions for easier viewing, reversed from their previous locations. The message center was moved down below the speedometer and added new functions such as a fog light indicator, air bag failure indicator, and the all-important "door ajar" warning.

Most Viper drivers would probably maintain that the car's 10-cylinder symphony is sound system enough. But if the occupants do want to hear music, it takes a whopping amplifier and speakers to overcome the Viper's exhaust note. So Dodge upgraded the stereo to a 200-watt amp and six speakers, which actually do overpower the engine when cranked up.

The larger interior volume and large glass area of the coupe increased the load on the air conditioning system, so the GTS got a bigger blower and improved ducting with fewer obstructions, increasing airflow 20 percent in the climate control system. An "enhanced" mode blends recirculated air with fresh air from outside and boosts airflow by 50 percent over the maximum setting in the original car. ■

Inspired by the great racing cars of the 1960s, the Viper GTS Coupe featured an aluminum flip-open filler cap. The beautiful cap contributes to the coupe's retro-racer image and covers the conventional plastic screw-on cap underneath.

The coupe's unexpectedly practical and spacious hatch area is large enough to carry one of the car's enormous tires, in the event of a flat tire. *John Lamm*

Aside from the obvious addition of a fixed roof to the coupe, the GTS also added a NACA duct to the hood to direct cool air to the engine's intake and a pair of louvered vents over the wheels to draw hot air from the engine bay. These changes are reminiscent of endurance racing sports prototypes.

designers how to make the new block stiffer using cross-bolted main bearing caps. The new caps were not only stronger, the caps and bolts were 2 pounds lighter—each! All of the changes to the short-block assembly totaled 40 pounds in weight savings.

What is so great about a door handle? Until the 1996 coupe, Vipers had no external door handles. The coupe used electrically actuated switches that release the doors. The hatch opens conventionally, providing access to manual door releases in the event of power failure.

A revised fuel-injection system is fed by the duct in the center of the hood. To improve tractability, Viper engineers replaced the fuel injection linkage with a new single cable system that helps maintain synchronization of the throttle bodies and reduces throttle sensitivity just off idle.

Behind the engine, to cut down on clatter at idle, the clutch was replaced with a larger but lighter one, featuring a damper that makes it quieter at idle.

A smaller 650 CCA battery replaced the 770 CCA cell in the original car to save weight, but a more powerful 143-amp alternator helps ensure there is enough power to run the new accessories and start the car.

The GTS Coupe arrived without the original car's side pipes, routing the exhaust out the back instead. This meant the car could use freer-flowing mufflers and still pass EPA noise requirements, so the change contributed to additional power. It also required insulating the back of the car from the fierce heat of the V-10's breath. This view also highlights the shocking width of the Viper's rear tires.

One obvious change on the GTS was the rear exhaust. The switch was made partly because of tighter emissions rules and the limitations of technology available at the time. Technology has since caught up, which is why the 2003 Viper returns to the original side-exhaust configuration.

"There was always a desire to have side exhaust," said Sjoberg. "The only reason we went to rear exhaust was that in 1996 when we had to go to [EPA emissions specification] OBD-II, the oxygen sensor must be rearward of the muffler. There was no way NGK could make an oxygen sensor that was both waterproof and temperature-resistant. The temperature-resistant oxygen sensors, which were ceramic, were not waterproof. The sill is a wet area as well as a very hot area. So you've either got a sensor that would be fine in temperature but would die in the presence of moisture, or vice versa.

"We had to go to a rear exhaust where we could put the sensor back in the rear wheelwell where it is removed far enough from the heat. To get adequate noise reduction, to meet the wide-open-throttle drive-by test, required substantial restriction in the muffler. That did two things. It cut down horsepower, and the more restriction the more the air stays there and the hotter it gets.

One wing provides lift and the other creates downforce. The coupe's superior aerodynamics and additional downforce challenged the suspension and tire engineers to develop a combination that worked well on both the coupe and the roadster. The Cessna's tires and suspension have little effect on its performance.

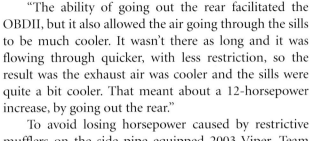

"The ability of going out the rear facilitated the OBDII, but it also allowed the air going through the sills to be much cooler. It wasn't there as long and it was flowing through quicker, with less restriction, so the result was the exhaust air was cooler and the sills were quite a bit cooler. That meant about a 12-horsepower increase, by going out the rear."

To avoid losing horsepower caused by restrictive mufflers on the side pipe equipped 2003 Viper, Team Viper pioneered active noise-canceling mufflers. The electronic mufflers introduce no back pressure, so the engine produces power as if it had no mufflers at all.

Routing the exhaust out the back created challenges, because the rear of the car hadn't been hardened against the Viper's prodigious heat output. Parts that had worked fine on the roadster failed in coupe prototypes.

"I was doing several days of tire tests at Road Atlanta in a test mule," said Michelin tire engineer Ken Payne. "I'd finished about four laps and commented over the radio that this set seemed to have gone away rather suddenly at the rear, stepping out more than expected under power out of turn seven. This looseness continued for the next hot lap and my cool-down lap.

"I motored into the pits fairly quickly to let [tire designer] Chris Baker get tire temps. The car stops, Chris starts to check tire temps, gets to the back of the car and then quite emphatically says 'Get out of the car NOW!' It turns out the slipping was due to a fuel leak! The prototype plastic fuel tank had gotten too hot, sagged down, and was rubbing over the differential. Fuel was running out at a pretty brisk rate. Perhaps that explained the fuel smell I had noticed a couple of times during that set of laps."

The suspension changes, as well as different weight distribution and new aerodynamics, meant the Viper needed a new set of tires to match the new parameters.

"We had started off with the XGTZ performance tire for the Viper," said Payne. "At the time, it was spot-on for what the car needed. By the time the coupe was going to launch in 1996, the market had evolved considerably, and noise and wet performance took on a little more importance.

Left
The coupe didn't just look really cool and go faster than the original roadster, it was also the foundation of a new Viper racing program. The Viper GTS-R (left) joined the coupe and roadster in the lineup in 1997 as an all-out racing model.

Above
Team Viper packs interesting technology into details such as the headlights on this coupe. Since 1996, Vipers have used halogen infrared reflective (HIR) bulbs that are brighter than conventional halogen bulbs, but much less expensive than high-intensity discharge (HID) headlights.

The Viper is more than a boulevard poseur, but it can do just that too, turning heads at sidewalk cafes.

"We knew that we needed to smooth off some of the rough edges of performance. The car's performance was staggering, but it also was a little bit of a knife-edge. With the coupe coming out, and knowing that the audience there was probably not going to be folks that were necessarily the Lotus Seven or Cobra sort of set, we wanted to put a little refinement in the manners of the car, particularly in the wet and at the limit. That led us to the next-generation tire, which launched on the coupe, then got carried over into the roadster.

"[The suspension changes] were directionally the right way to go. Throughout the development of the car, we worked really closely with Team Viper, keeping abreast of what they were doing. We have some vehicle measurement capabilities and labs here at Michelin. We would feed back information as to what we thought were good directions to move in terms of suspension and vehicle changes. That was all very positive. We were quite pleased by the rework of the suspension when the coupe came out.

"The aerodynamic package of the coupe planted things quite well. It did present an interesting challenge for us, in that the coupe and roadster were quite different in their behavior at higher speeds because of aerodynamics. We had to work really carefully to get a tire package that was nice on both cars.

"We didn't want to bias the tire so it would be great on one car and hurt the performance of the other. We wanted both cars to have a touch of steady-state understeer at the limit, because that, for the average person, is certainly the preferred balance of the vehicle.

"But we still wanted them close enough to neutral that when you wanted to drive them in a spirited manner, it came across well. That was one of those unique situations where you had some inherent differences between the coupe and the roadster that challenged us to walk that fine line to

While some accused the Viper roadster of having the aerodynamics of a house, the sleek GTS Coupe smoothed that out considerably. The roadster's .50 coefficient of drag wasn't hard to beat, but the coupe's .39 score was good, considering the car's massive width, huge tires, and large spoiler. More important than drag, though, is the coupe's aerodynamic downforce, which gives the car stability at speeds that would be hair-raising in the roadster.

get the tires just right. We walked back and forth with that a lot, testing both platforms to make sure that in the end, the product worked equally well on both cars."

John Herlitz had said, "The inspiration for the Cobra Daytona Coupe was the Cobra Roadster. It was a closed car to go to Le Mans with and of course it won at Le Mans. As such it became an icon of successful American racing in Europe."

Could he also have been talking about the Viper?

The introduction of the original Viper RT/10 was a press-relations landmark. Chrysler Corporation successfully held the attention of journalists for three years, from the concept car's introduction at the North American International Auto Show in Detroit in 1989 until the production car's debut there in 1992. During that time, journalists sat in on product meetings and were shown sneak previews of development prototypes. The Viper paced the 1991 Indy 500 seven months before it was introduced. The result was a steady stream of favorable articles and attention-getting magazine covers.

And by the time the cars were in customers' hands, the process had stretched to four years. "We had a three-year communications plan in place to keep Viper visible," said Tom Kowaleski, who was then the Viper PR person, but we had four years of great events and great actions. It started in the summer of '89 when we announced we were going to go and do it. We did four events and each one had a consistent message and a new message for each event."

The launch of the RT/10 was meant as a baptism into the family of American sports cars, taking place at that memorable party at Phil Hill's place, with the likes of Dan Gurney, Parnelli Jones, and

Carroll Shelby in attendance. So, for the launch of the GTS Coupe in 1996, Chrysler faced the challenge of matching the media barrage they had pulled off with the original Viper. This was made more difficult by the fact that the Viper was beginning to suffer from exposure, at least to the jaded journalists.

It was no secret that Chrysler intended to take the Viper racing. The first hint might have come when Carroll Shelby drove the prototype as the pace car in the 1991 Indy 500. And by the time the GTS was introduced, it became fairly clear that racing was what it was about.

Said Kowaleski, "We started to think about, how do you take this American sports car and put it into an international perspective? How can we use the launch program for its international intent?"

The Viper had been successfully positioned as the heir to the tradition of American sports cars and musclecars. But now the coupe would step onto the world stage, taking on the world's best,

The American Club Racing Viper is built for speed, but the car is comfortable enough for a leisurely ride in the country. A low-restriction air filter boosts rated horsepower to 460 and torque to 500 foot-pounds.

The coupe made a splashy arrival, serving as pace car for the 1996 Indianapolis 500 race on Memorial Day weekend. The event kicked off the world press introduction of the car, which continued in Europe the following week.

Porsche and Ferrari, not only on the street, but on the track too. A Viper GTS had qualified for the upcoming 24 Hours of Le Mans.

So Kowaleski used the company's entry into racing as the theme for the launch of the GTS. It was the press launch of the millennium.

"We went to European circuits to show the car," said Kowaleski. "Not just any European circuits, but ones where Americans had distinguished themselves. We started at Weisbaden, went to Nurburgring, and drove on the old circuit, then had a great drive that afternoon across Belgium in the Ardennes. The next day we drove on the original circuit and the new circuit at Spa. Then we went to Champagne and put the cars on the old GP circuit at Reims."

Finally came Paris, resulting in the now-famous images of the Vipers driving three-abreast through the heart of the City of Lights. "We drove down Champs Elysees. It wasn't planned; it just happened. Everybody was grabbing their cameras. We knew if we asked the police for an escort it would never happen, so we just did it."

Again, Chrysler invited racing icons. "We brought [American Formula 1 World Champion] Phil Hill, [famed racing photographer] Jesse Alexander, and [sports car ace] Brian Redmond. We'd have a chalk talk, and they'd talk about reminiscences of the circuit. It was priceless. This was really, really a lot of fun."

The Chrysler media team left no detail unattended. The goal was to overwhelm writers with history while driving the GTS Coupe, and it worked.

Recalled journalist Bob Storck, "The really remarkable thing was that not only did we have Sjoberg and Castaing and people of that nature on this thing, we had Jesse and Phil giving us these marvelous fill-ins. Pete Brock, who was the progenitor of the Cobra Daytona

Formula One champion Phil Hill went with the U.S. press corps on the launch of the Viper GTS Coupe, describing the tracks that they would visit and giving scribes rides in the cars so they could see how fast a pro could make the new Viper go.

The Spa-Francorchamps circuit in Belgium is composed of public roads. Here, a Viper GTS Coupe accelerates through the infamous Eu Rouge curve, in its role as two-lane highway.

The Nurburgring is another fearsomely fast track. The Viper proved to be right at home on the track's famed north loop, which is no longer used for racing. *John Lamm*

coupe, he was icing on the cake. I managed to sit at a lot of dinners with those three guys, and it was priceless."

More than fun, more than priceless. Recalled *Popular Mechanics* writer Mike Allen, "It was the press trip of the millennium.

"It started off with a chance to go to the Indy 500 and to get a lap around the track in the [Viper GTS Coupe] pace car with Johnny Rutherford driving," he said. "When you got off the plane in Indianapolis someone met you at baggage claim, took your bags away, and then took you out to the parking lot, where there were a dozen red Viper convertibles to drive for the next day or two.

"We stayed in a hotel outside of town. Significant others were invited, so I took my girlfriend. There were dinners and things to do, but pretty much the whole event was structured around going to the racetrack.

"There was the Indy 500 black tie banquet, the high point of which was introduction of the Indy 500 queen, who is basically the winner of the local Indy 500 contest in every high school in the whole state of Indiana. It was definitely Americana.

"Then we went to Germany, where there were 18 Viper coupes," said Allen. "All of these cars had prototype VINs on them. They probably went into a crusher somewhere. What a shame.

"We had a fantastic meal, got a little rest in the afternoon, and headed out to the track the next morning. I think it was Nurburgring.

"The whole agenda was, we'd start out with a cocktail reception the evening before with Jesse Alexander and Phil Hill. We'd sit around in the bar with a slide projector, and Jesse Alexander would show us a tray full of slides of photographs he had taken during the Phil Hill era in Formula One. And all of them would be of one particular racetrack. So Jesse and Phil would trade war stories for about an hour, and then we'd have dinner. The next morning we'd drive to that racetrack and go turn hot laps.

"We went to Nurburgring. We went to Spa. We went to four or five racetracks all told, in sequence. It was the same drill. Every afternoon we'd meet for a couple of beers and the slide show and then have dinner. Then we'd get up the next morning and tour to whatever that racetrack was the night before. I must say they did not go out of their way to find two-star hotels for us. They were all pretty nice places."

Said Bob Storck, "Of all the tracks we drove at in Europe, the one that truly blew me away was Reims. It was just an amazing thing to be out there driving hard on nothing more than French country roads and realize this was the way the race had run.

"One of the people I drove around with was Francois Castaing," he said. "The little town of Gue was the only slow point on the entire course, two 120-degree turns. Everything else was just really fast sweepers with ditches on either side of the road.

"Here I was flailing up this road with Francois sitting next to me. He is kind of guiding me with his hands and urging me to run all the way out to the edge of the road. And I am sitting there thinking, 'If I killed Francois Castaing, I'm never going to get invited back to another Chrysler trip.' "

The press event of the millennium concluded with an impromptu parade through Paris, like something out of a movie.

Said Allen, "The last morning we got up and drove a considerable distance into Paris and drove the 18 Viper coupes, in echelon, three wide, six rows, up and down the Champs Elysees from the Eiffel Tower to the Place de la Concord. In the photos, I'm driving the car on the right-front corner. The people were lined up six deep on the curb. It was bitchin'."

"That was the day we had been to Reims," said Storck. "We got to Paris and we lined up. About this time I was talking to [Chrysler PR person] Rex Greenslade and said, 'Do we have police escort?' and he said he found it was better not to tell the police what they were doing.

"This was all extremely unofficial. This was at two o'clock on a Friday afternoon, and it was just packed with cars and we just kind of inched down. The whole idea was they were going to make just a line of the 18 cars down the Champs. That really wasn't going to work.

Right
Belgian road signs point the way toward the local racing mecca. In the years since this press event, the quintessentially American Viper has made itself quite at home at most of Europe's most famous circuits. *John Lamm*

Above
The faded garages at Reims, France, stand in contrast to the shiny new Vipers. The old track is used only as a public road now. *John Lamm*

"We got up to the Place de la Concorde and turned around, and someone made the suggestion we go into three abreast. When we did that, we were just unstoppable. There was a big phalanx of cars that went down the Champs, all together, nobody could get in, nobody would intrude. There was such an amazing variety of reactions from the crowd. The vast majority looked on in curiosity and amazement and that French sort of look of curiosity and disdain. There were big clumps that would be clapping and waving. One of the beauties was the car was blue [the French national color].

"One thing that I'll always recall is that there was this cute little French girl on a bicycle, and who, since we were in kind of heavy traffic, she was able to work her way up the line. She was riding with short shorts and a big smile on her face and pumping one arm up and down. She thought this was really fun.

"A lot of the really good pictures were taken by Pete Brock, who was standing on top of the minivan that was leading the bunch. To me, that was really one of the really amusing and amazing things, was to watch Pete Brock like this overage surfer."

Said Brock, "It was really one of the most exciting things to do. At that time nobody had even really even seen a Viper in Europe, much less seen one on the street. People had seen pictures of them in magazines, but it was a spaceship when it landed. It was just incredibly exciting to see them all rolling down the road. As we began to form up, the Parisians sort of

Vipers take Paris! A phalanx of journalists in Vipers successfully penetrated Paris traffic, creating no small commotion along the way. Viper PR guys knew that attempting to coordinate with French police for an organized parade would be unproductive, so they had an impromptu one instead.

Objective achieved. The Viper parade reached the Champs Elysees in formation, despite choking local traffic. *John Lamm*

got behind the whole thing and let us in for this impromptu parade. We were running three abreast down the street.

"I got up on top of a van in front of the whole thing as we went down the road and got these images that were just fabulous. It was some of the best stuff that I shot at the time. With all the Parisian traffic around it, it is obvious that nothing is blocked off. This is the real thing happening. You could see the Arc de Triomphe in the back and the Parisian cars and buses and people.

"The traffic was so thick that bicycles and stuff were still going along. Here comes this gal in this bright yellow sweater on a bicycle pedaling down the street. I motioned her over to get into it. She kind of wheeled in with this bicycle in front of all of these things. It was a great little bit of color of Paris to have that little thing happen like that. It turned out to be a great shot."

"We had dinner at the Automobile Club of France," said Allen. "The Viper GTS Coupe that had just qualified at Le Mans a couple [of] days before was parked at the curb out front. And I mean right straight off the racetrack, with duct tape and bugs and things all over it."

Despite the incredible impression left by the unbelievable events of the introduction, those who attended were a bit reluctant to reveal just how incredible the event really was. "I came back and tried to kind of downplay it a little bit because I'd have every guy that I know wanting to become an automotive journalist," said Storck.

CHAPTER SIX

MAKING HISTORY

Vipers are hand-built in DaimlerChrysler's Conner Avenue assembly plant, one of the few such plants in the world. Each car is built from about 50 component modules, so heavy industrial work, such as stamping, casting, machining, painting, and welding, takes place elsewhere.

The Viper is built on a line with only 31 workstations. The cars spend the better part of an hour at each station, where human hands carefully perform a variety of tasks. Chrysler calls its Viper-builders "craftspersons," because of the performance level expected of them. Each craftsperson gets 300 hours of training to prepare him or her for the important job of assembling the Viper.

After nearly a decade of getting finished engines from an engine plant, Conner Avenue now assembles Viper engines too.

"We're the only assembly plant in North America that builds their own engines," said John Hinckley, the plant's recently retired manager. "We have the engine assembly line across the aisle from the chassis line, where the engine is installed into the frame. We have small groups of people building Viper engines at eight engines a day. We start with a raw block and all of the components are purchased finished, ready to assemble. We're really excited about that. We have the heart of the car right here, and that is what people buy the car for."

The Conner Avenue plant that produces Vipers is not only flexible enough to assemble both Coupes and Roadsters on the same line, but it also built the prototypes for the 2003 Viper, assembles Prowlers, and even builds its own engines. John Lamm

99

The Conner Avenue plant may be the picture of a clean, modern, efficient low-volume manufacturing site, but it wasn't that way just a few years ago. Viper assembly started off inside another manufacturing plant, New Mack Assembly, before moving into the "spark plug plant."

"The Viper plant was originally down at New Mack Viper assembly back in '92, when production started," Hinckley said. "About the middle of '95, we were notified we had to get out of that building because they were going to convert it into a new engine plant. It's the plant today that produces the 4.7-liter V-8 for the Grand Cherokee and the Dakota, among other things.

"So we scrambled around and found the building we're in now, which was built in 1966 by Champion Spark Plugs. It was probably the shortest, fastest refurbishment of an old building and conversion of it into an assembly plant anyone has ever seen. It ran for about 20 years and made the porcelain insulators for the Champion spark plugs that were shipped all over the world. Champion closed the plant in about 1986, and it just sat here empty for about nine years. Except in the meantime, everybody in Detroit who had some kind of machine tool to store wound up storing it here.

"We found the building and bought it right near the end of June 1995. Then we hired about every contractor we could find in the city of Detroit and set them up on a seven-day-a-week, 24-hour schedule. They proceeded to clear out and refurbish the plant and get it ready to bring the Viper tooling up from about 3 miles down the road. It took about 720 50-foot flatbed semis to haul all of the junk out of here before we could even start to refurbish the building. Probably the hardest part was getting the building clear, getting all of the stored machine tools and junk out of it. A lot of it, we didn't even know who it belonged to.

"With all that stuff in the building, it made it hard to assess the actual condition of the building and what it would need in terms of refurbishment. Because of the fact that the primary product here

The bare Viper frame begins its trip down the assembly line, the start of its journey to becoming a Viper the next day. *Alfredo Passarelli, courtesy of DaimlerChrysler Corporation*

The exhaust header and heat shield are installed as the completed V-10 engine is prepared for installation in the car. *Alfredo Passarelli, courtesy of DaimlerChrysler Corporation*

The windshield cowl detours onto its own mini-assembly line for installation of the dashboard components such as the instrument cluster, HVAC controls, and the stereo. This is before the finished assembly is reinstalled in the chassis on the main assembly line. *Alfredo Passarelli, courtesy of DaimlerChrysler Corporation*

The cast-aluminum upper control arms are installed, as the lower control arms droop from their mounts below. *Alfredo Passarelli, courtesy of DaimlerChrysler Corporation*

All of the Viper's beautiful aluminum suspension components are visible, as the steering spindle is bolted to the lower control arm. Notice the black strut that holds the suspension in place, because the shock absorber and spring assembly haven't been installed yet. *Alfredo Passarelli, courtesy of DaimlerChrysler Corporation*

was porcelain insulator[s], the building was absolutely filled with talcum powder dust. There was talcum powder dust everywhere. I can't tell you how many power washings and cleanings it took to make the rear second floor part of the building anywhere near habitable.

"We started that right about the first week of July. We hauled everything out of here, refurbished the building, went through the mechanical and electrical systems, and cleaned everything up, painted it, and got it ready to bring the tooling up here. We brought the tooling in and in late September we were building Vipers here. We launched the '96 Viper roadster here, right near the end of September. It was quite a project. There are still 10 huge silos standing behind the plant that used to be full of talcum powder."

Now, with the shock and spring installed, the antisway bar link is bolted to the lower control arm. *Alfredo Passarelli, courtesy of DaimlerChrysler Corporation*

The differential, which must withstand the V-10 engine's torrid output, is readied for installation in the chassis. *Alfredo Passarelli, courtesy of DaimlerChrysler Corporation*

Hinckley takes a great deal of pride in the standards on the Viper line. "Because of the low volume, our conveyers don't move continuously," he said. "The car stays at each workstation for about 45 minutes. In a typical high-volume plant, the car enters and leaves the workstation in about 45 seconds. Here it enters the workstation and stops. Generally there are two people in a workstation, and those two craftspersons work on that car for 45 minutes.

"So they are essentially doing about 50 times the work content on that car that a team would do in a high-volume plant. That requires a lot of parts on the line, a lot of tools, a lot of expertise, a lot of skills. That's why we call them craftspersons. It takes a while to learn a job that has 45 minutes of work content as well.

With the chassis lifted into the air, the differential, driveshaft, and exhaust system are installed. *Alfredo Passarelli, courtesy of DaimlerChrysler Corporation*

Right
The previously dry Viper receives its vital fluids, such as oil, hydraulic fluid, and coolant. *Alfredo Passarelli, courtesy of DaimlerChrysler Corporation*

"You can teach someone to do a high-volume plant assembly job probably in about 25 minutes. Here it takes a week or two to learn the job, because there is so much content.

"Most of the people here come from other Detroit-area Chrysler plants," Hinckley said. "When we need people, we post notices in their plants. The applications go to our human resources center and go through a battery of tests. The ones that get through that testing procedure come to us, and we interview them here and select the ones we would like to bring in. Those people go in a pool. They are identified as having been screened and having been qualified to work here. Then the next time we need people, those are the first people who are transferred. It is a very selective process because our requirements are different than a high-volume plant. Just because somebody has worked at another Chrysler plant for 20 years doesn't mean they can transfer in here. They can only come in here if they meet our requirements."

An early priority with the craftspersons was to make the assembly process as efficient as possible.

Said Hinckley, "One of the most significant changes we made, after we got the line up and running here, is how we subassembled the cowl assembly. That comes in as part of the frame, but we remove it from the frame and subassemble all the instrument panel, steering wheel, and air conditioning, and all of the electronics to it before it goes back on the frame on the main line.

"That subassembly process used to be kind of an in-line process, where this big bulky part was placed in a fixture and then some work was done on it, then it was picked up by an overhead hoist and transferred to another fixture. That process went through about four lift-and-carry stations for subassembly, and it didn't work out very well. It was difficult to display the material, it took time to carry it between stations, and it wasn't very efficient.

Upper right
The machine checks the alignment of all four wheels simultaneously. Alignment of a Viper's suspension is critical, because of the width of the tires and because it pays to know where a 450-horsepower car is pointed at all times. Like Ferrari, Team Viper checks bump steer to make sure the car doesn't change direction when it hits bumps. *Alfredo Passarelli, courtesy of DaimlerChrysler Corporation*

"So we had a workshop with the folks that work in that area and said, 'All right, what's a better way to do this job?' After a three-day workshop that examined the layout and all the parts and the assembly sequence, the folks that worked in the area came up with the idea of a four-station round carousel process on a big rotating fixture instead of going in line from one fixture to another. It is much more efficient, it is easier to display the material on the line, and there is a lot less walking involved.

"All in all it is a much more ergonomically attractive arrangement. In addition, it reduced the manpower required by about 20 percent because the layout was much more efficient. And I think, more important than anything else, it worked very well because it was designed by the people who worked in the area and they had ownership of it."

"I thought they did a good, pragmatic job on the design of the whole assembly process," said Bob Storck, an engineer and veteran journalist who is familiar with the Viper plant. "They had a problem with taking a lot of components built off loose tooling and putting them together and wanting some level of reasonable fit and finish. What they did was to come up with a check station that I haven't seen the likes of anywhere else.

"They would take the components, say the basic frame, mount it in there, go through some electronic checks that measured where the critical points were, then they would drop in a center section and measure it up. They would drop in a hood. What they would come up with was a set of readings that would enable them to pick the right shim packs for the right locations that would bring everything into line. I thought it was a very nice approach."

"There is a great deal of finesse involved in getting all the panels to fit," agrees Hinckley. "There is a lot of handwork in the parts, so you see more dimensional variation than you might see in a

The Viper's massive wheel and tire assemblies are installed using a machine that tightens and torques all six lug nuts at once. *Alfredo Passarelli, courtesy of DaimlerChrysler Corporation*

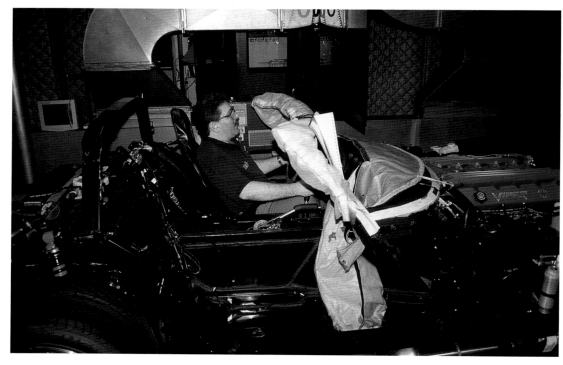

A stripped-down Viper hot rod: The engine is started and the rolling chassis is tested on the dynomometer to verify performance and check for leaks. *Alfredo Passarelli, courtesy of DaimlerChrysler Corporation*

This roadster's chassis receives its rally bar, which is bolted and glued into place to provide additional structural rigidity. *Alfredo Passarelli, courtesy of DaimlerChrysler Corporation*

Team Viper uses a precise jig system that ensures correct alignment of body parts as they are installed on the frame. As production tolerances improve for the 2003 Viper, these jogs won't be as critical for ensuring a quality assembly. *Alfredo Passarelli, courtesy of DaimlerChrysler Corporation*

typical part. So we're set up to deal with that. Each person along the line, part of their job is to do whatever is necessary to make sure that parts fit just right. That might require reaming of holes, it may require some filing, it may require some shims, it may require any number of little finesse operations in order to get the part to fit just right. That is just part of building a low-volume car. Each car is a little different and that is part of the skill set required to be a craftsperson at Conner Avenue Assembly and that is what those folks do best."

They do it so well, in fact, that they have attracted attention from another group tasked with assembling an image-building low-volume car: the Mercedes-Benz Maybach. That will be a Mercedes ultra-high-end luxury sedan, designed to take on Rolls-Royce. The car will be built in extremely low volumes, so people on the Mercedes side of the company have taken an interest in the former Chrysler Corporation's experience with such production.

"We've had some contact with the people who will be doing the Maybach," said Hinckley. "Their team has been in here a couple [of] times. We know them pretty well."

Even Mercedes "tuner" cars, built by AMG, are built in higher volumes than the Viper or the Maybach. And those cars are upgraded, rather than assembled from scratch, so Mercedes couldn't find much help in examining AMG, Hinckley said.

Viper craftspersons build eight Vipers a day, with each car taking three and a half days. "It takes about a day and a half on the chassis line, before it gets roll-tested, then it's about two days to go down the final line," said Hinckley.

The assembly procedure starts with a bare frame, supplied by outside contractor Fabco. "The frame is made up of cross-sections of steel tubing and sheet metal and a lot of hand welding," Hinckley said. "They build the frame and then they send it to another firm, which cleans it and then dip-primes it and bakes it."

"We take that frame and pull the cowl assembly off it. The cowl assembly goes into that carousel subassembly where the instrument panel, air conditioning, electronics, and pedals are installed. Meanwhile, the frame the cowl came off of goes onto the main line. It goes up in the air and gets all the plumbing and the brake and fuel lines and the wiring that is underneath the car.

"The differential goes on and then the frame moves forward another station. The cowl assembly comes back out of that carousel subassembly, goes back onto that frame. At that point we begin to put the suspension components on the car, the front and rear control arms, and spindles and hubs. Then we finish up with the brakes.

"Then the engine is picked up and put into the car with the transmission on it. After the engine goes in, then the radiator support, radiator, air conditioning condenser, and the engine oil cooler. We finish up the shift boot where the shift lever comes through the floor, put the fuel tank on.

"Then we have one overhead station the car goes into where we button up underneath the car, finish up the exhaust system, the catalytic converters, the resonators, the mufflers, and all the rear pipes. We put the transmission tunnel plate on the bottom. It is a big aluminum plate that closes off the bottom of the tunnel.

"Then the car is put into a specially designed alignment machine, where we set caster, camber, and toe at both ends. With the 13-inch-wide tires, the camber angle is extremely critical. We have the

Like the rally bar, the rear fenders are also permanently installed on the chassis. Because all of the Viper's body parts are prepainted, workers use extreme care when handling them to avoid scratching the paint. *Alfredo Passarelli, courtesy of DaimlerChrysler Corporation*

The Viper's steel doorsills are insulated (the shiny foil on the red doorsill) to deflect exhaust heat from the mufflers that reside under the car's doorjambs. *Alfredo Passarelli, courtesy of DaimlerChrysler Corporation*

The windshield frame receives sealant in preparation for the windshield's installation in this nearly finished coupe. *Alfredo Passarelli, courtesy of DaimlerChrysler Corporation*

Underhood weatherstripping proved to be critical during wet-weather tire testing in protecting the ignition system from the spray off the front tires. *Alfredo Passarelli, courtesy of DaimlerChrysler Corporation*

most advanced alignment machine on the planet. It was built specifically for the Viper, and it sets camber for both the front and the rear within 2/100ths of a degree.

"We do another thing that is unusual that nobody else other than Ferrari does, and that is we set bump steer on the front end. We measure the toe change at both jounce and rebound, and we shim the mounting of the steering gear to the frame in order to zero-out the bump steer on the front end.

"When it comes off the alignment machine, we put wheels and tires on, set it on the floor, and then fire the engine for the first time. We fill it with fluids; the only automation in the entire plant is fluid filling. We use typical evacuate-and fill equipment, similar to what you'd find in a

Preparation and installation of the Viper's enormous clamshell hood is one of the most labor-intensive parts of the car's construction. The large hood is difficult to handle while installing the insulation and weatherstripping. *Alfredo Passarelli, courtesy of DaimlerChrysler Corporation*

high-volume plant, that evacuates and fills the coolant, the brake fluid, power steering fluid, and air conditioning refrigerant.

"Once it has got fluids in it, we fire the engine for the first time. That is the first time the engine has been hot-fired. We fire it up and take it into the roll-test booth, and spend about 12 minutes in the roll-test booth exercising the car. We run it back and forth up to about 90 miles an hour and down, checking out the antilock brake system of the car and the air conditioning system. It is a fully functional car at that point, although it is just a chassis. Normally, the roll-test of the car is the last thing that is done after it comes off the assembly line, but here it is in the middle of the process.

"After we roll-test it, we certify it mechanically and dynamically as a chassis. Then the car is inspected very carefully for any leaks. The safety fasteners for brakes, suspension, and steering are all double-checked. Then it goes on the final line and gets the interior and exterior body skins put on it.

"The first part that goes on is the rear clip, which is a large fiberglass assembly that forms the foundation of the rear half of the body. You don't see it when the car is complete, but it forms the foundation for the rear quarters and the deck lid and the roof. That rear clip, which is different for the roadster and the coupe, is both bolted on and bonded to the frame with a two-part Goodyear adhesive. It is the same adhesive that is used to put wing skins on airplanes. When that part goes on, it becomes a structural part that is not about to be removed.

"Once the rear clip is on, we start trimming out the interior. We finish the interior before we start putting the roof or any body panels on it because it is easier to get at and easier to work in. The carpeting goes in, the rear bulkhead trim panels go in, the seatbelts go in, the seats, the center console, and all the interior trim is done.

"Once the interior is complete, the process differs a little between the coupe and the roadster. If it's a coupe, the roof goes on first. It is bolted and bonded on, so it becomes a structural member as well, then the rear quarter panels are installed, and the rear finishing panel that has the taillights in it.

Mounting the hood on its hinges and then installing the latches and strikers completes the process. *Alfredo Passarelli, courtesy of DaimlerChrysler Corporation*

A few bits of trim and weatherstripping are the final details in the Viper's construction. *Alfredo Passarelli, courtesy of DaimlerChrysler Corporation*

Unlike most new cars, Vipers leave the factory looking like new cars. That means any smudges the car might have picked up are wiped clean, and the car's finish is buffed to a brilliant shine. *Alfredo Passarelli, courtesy of DaimlerChrysler Corporation*

"If it's a roadster, the first body panel that goes on is what we call the sport cap. That is the big panel behind the seats that looks like a big painted roll bar. It is followed by the rear quarter panels and then the rear deck lid.

"Then, as the car goes down the line, it picks up the headliner, windshield, and then the doors. The doors are built up right adjacent to the line and subassembled with the glass and the mechanicals and then the doors are hung and fitted on the car. The next station down the line, the hood goes on. The hood is subassembled off-line with the insulator pad and hinges and rollers and sliders. It goes on the car and gets fitted.

"The next station is a lift station. It goes up on a hoist and the front and rear fender liners, splash shields if you will, are installed and then the front and rear fascias are installed, along with the headlights. Then it comes back down and we put the inner door trim panels on, and fire it up and drive it off the line. At that point it's a complete car, except for aiming the headlights and water-testing it.

"The finished paint specification on a Viper is 'show paint,'" said Hinckley. "It has absolutely the finest paint finish on it that you can get on any car, anywhere, and we take great pains to make sure that we don't damage it as we assemble it. Then when the car is done, the last thing that happens to it before it goes through final inspection is about a two-hour detailing treatment, which includes a complete buff, glaze, and polish on every square inch of the outside of the car to literally a mirror finish. That is kind of a hallmark of the Viper, its incredible paint finish."

CHAPTER SEVEN

RACING

The 1992 RT/10 roadster may have started a new chapter in the history of Chrysler and sports cars, but it didn't cause the likes of Porsche and Ferrari much concern over the Viper taking over their racing territory. By 1996, it was beginning to. By 2000, it had.

But in the 1994 debut at Le Mans, two Viper roadsters, with hard tops added, were entered by the French Rent-a-Car team. Drivers Justin Bell, Rene Arnoux, and Bertand Balas finished 10th overall and third in class.

"That was the astounding thing," said Bell. "You know, we finished 10th overall. That is amazing. It took the factory team another two years to do that."

Bell suggested, however, that the high finish had more to do with attrition than the speed of the car. "It was still two years before the factory decided to go with a proper car, so it was a road car," he said. "It was doing 190 miles per hour and the front was lifting off the road, almost flipping. It was very scary. And it had a false roof on it. The heat of the car, oh! We were in Japan one year, it was 65 [degrees Celsius, or 150 degrees Fahrenheit] in our car!"

When the GTS Coupe was developed, with its lighter suspension, stiffer chassis, stronger engine, and better aerodynamics, Team Viper had the weapon it needed. Victory at Le Mans was the goal.

If Team Viper strategists had plotted a dream scenario, they'd have been unlikely to predict racing accomplishments so dominant as the Viper has achieved on the world's most famous tracks. Endurance racing is where world-class sports cars make world-class reputations for excellence. The Viper won the FIA GT2 championships in 1997 and 1998, and then won the reclassified FIA GT championship in 1999. It won the American Le Mans Series GTS Teams title and the Driver's and Manufacturer's Championships in 1999, running only five of eight races, winning them all.

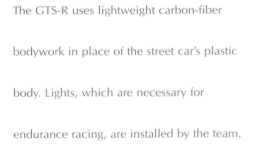

The GTS-R uses lightweight carbon-fiber bodywork in place of the street car's plastic body. Lights, which are necessary for endurance racing, are installed by the team.

But Le Mans was the Holy Grail. In 1998, factory-supported GTS-R Vipers campaigned by the French team ORECA finished first and second in GT2 at Le Mans. Many magnums of champagne, in both Paris and Detroit, must have flowed that night.

In 1999 the ORECA cars again finished one-two, with privateers finishing third through sixth.

But 2000, the last year of Dodge factory Viper GTS-R racing, was a hell of a swan song. A Viper won the 24 Hours of Daytona, overall. Daytona had never been won by an American production-based sports car. Then the team went to Sebring, where Vipers finished first, second, and third. And then Le Mans: first, second, fourth.

After winning consecutive FIA GT Championships in European road racing, the Viper's racing pedigree was quickly and forcefully established to its toughest audience. Dozens of Chrysler Vipers were sold in Europe (they were badged Chrysler because Dodge isn't sold there), first as gray-market cars imported from America and then full-on Euro-certified cars. In England, France, Germany, and even Japan, new Viper Club of America (VCA) chapters were springing up across the globe like mushrooms after a spring rain.

In 1995, Dodge released its factory-built race car, available to teams for sports car racing. The GTS-R is the blank canvas upon which racing teams can paint their skill and sponsors' colors, in search of victory. The base engine in the GTS-R produces 525 horsepower, but 650-horsepower and 750-horsepower versions are available.

The GTS-R race cars are built in the same plant by the same Team Viper "craftspersons" as standard-production Vipers, accelerating the transfer of racing technology to the production cars. Just as important, the team transferred a can-do spirit and awareness to the engineers and craftspersons who rotated through the program.

Above right
The V-10 thunder that poured out of the Viper GTS-R's unmuffled side pipes captured the attention and imagination of fans around the world.

"The Viper got a lot of television coverage," said Bob Lutz. "The races are always on television in Europe on Eurosport, and they get high ratings. The camera crews focus a lot on the Vipers, because they look different and they sound different. When they've got these telephoto shots of the Vipers charging up into corners, it's these big hulking monsters with heat waves shimmering off them. It's sensational photography. When they photograph these slippery Audis where everything kind of looks the same, it's not nearly as exciting.

"I sold my original blue GTS to my son-in-law in Switzerland," Lutz added. "When he drove it home through his residential area, he emptied out the schoolyard. Kids were running down the street shouting, 'It's the Viper race car, it's the Viper race car!'"

But image-building wasn't the only reason Team Viper went racing, said Roy Sjoberg. "We can sell every Viper we can make, so what's the point of racing, marketing and PR-wise? There's always a benefit in racing engineering development-wise, to continue to improve the breed. That's what we did with the original Viper.

"When we originally went racing, most of the racers we approached, from [Tom] Walkinshaw to [Rob] Dyson, just scoffed at us. They said, 'What do you mean, Chrysler is going sports car racing? You don't know anything about our race cars. I'll make a purpose-built race car and we'll make it kind of look like a Viper, and you'll get all of the PR and marketing benefit.'

"We weren't going to get any engineering development benefit, so I vetoed that. Now we've shown the vehicle has the durability, has the performance, has the capability to be a winner."

You've heard the expression "Racing improves the breed"? Well, Chrysler's racing program was designed to improve the breeders, who then would improve every Chrysler breed they touched. The plan was bold, progressive, and pure. The primary objective was to learn engineering; winning races was the bonus. Let the publicity chips fall where they may. The company was confident enough in its image and clear enough in its goals to dive into the deep end. "We might as well run with the big boys and see what happens," shrugged Neil Hanneman, development engineer for the GTS-R, and a four-time SCCA champion himself.

Above

The wind can be cruel to the unprepared, so Team Viper tested the GTS-R in the wind tunnel before building it, to guarantee proper aerodynamic downforce and balance.

Right inset

When all else fails, try a wing off a Boeing 777. Mounted upside down, of course.

Right

It took a couple of seasons to get the factory GTS-R fully developed, but when the wins started coming they didn't stop. The factory-backed French Team ORECA won Le Mans four times in a row, beginning with this car.

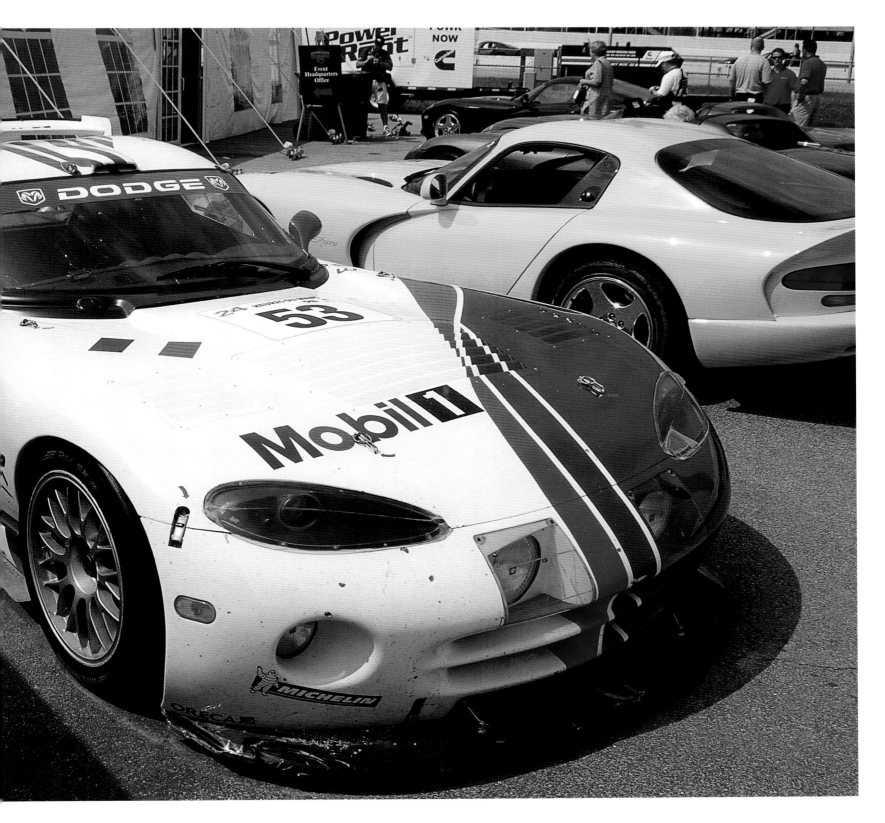

"We're the bang-for-the-buck guys," he said. "It's not win at all costs for us, it's efficiency we're after. There's a sense of urgency in racing that could reduce the development time of production cars. The idea is to train young designers and engineers, and then have them pollinate throughout the company. Chrysler wants the new guys to learn and make mistakes. That's part of the philosophy here."

Chrysler's own factory racing team was led by Hanneman, with two customer teams, Canaska/Southwind in Canada and Team ORECA in France. In early 1996 there were six GTS-Rs in existence, divided evenly among the three. The relationship between Chrysler and its two teams was close and generous. The line blurred in both budget and engineering. Chrysler engineers were assigned to the customer teams—as much to help Chrysler as the teams. Chrysler engineers concentrated on the engine, while the teams developed the chassis and suspension.

Viper drivers spent more time on victory podiums between 1997 and 2001 than anyone else. Pictured are David Donahue and Luca Drudi. *Justin Bell*

The new engine was designed with racing in mind, in particular the redesigned cooling system. "On the race engines we upped the thickness of the iron sleeve," said Roy Sjoberg. "We actually changed the bore of the aluminum casting so we could have a thicker-sleeved engine for the race engine. We were putting out over 700 horsepower, so we needed that for general durability.

"We had to back off on compression on the original engine because we couldn't cool it adequately to get the 10:1 compression ratio we wanted; we had some detonation," Sjoberg said. "When we went to the new casting, we totally changed the cooling jacket. That very much improved our ability to up compression ratios and do other things with it. For the race engine, which is made off that block, there were minor modifications relative to cooling."

If there was any secret to Viper's success, it was Hugues de Chaunac, who has been called the Roger Penske of France. He had founded team ORECA in 1973 when he was still a driver. Since then, his teams had taken titles in Formula 3, Formula 2, Formula 3000, and Formula Renault, had competed in Formula 1, and won Le Mans overall in 1991 running the Mazda factory prototype. To this, add rallying, desert, touring cars, and even ice racing. Drivers the likes of Alain Prost, Rene Arnoux, Jacques Laffite, Patrick Tambay, and Jean Alesi have been educated, groomed, and boosted to fame while driving for de Chaunac.

When Viper drivers weren't atop podiums, they were hard at work inside their cars. Even this "stock" Viper GTS-R has an imposing, all-business feel to the cockpit. *John Lamm*

Said Justin Bell, who moved from Rent-a-Car to ORECA, "The pace of the development of the Viper racing car was astounding. I have to credit team ORECA for that. Hugues de Chaunac ran a phenomenal team that had great engineers. I know they pushed Chrysler.

"The Chrysler corporate motorsports infrastructure was not set up to handle the speed of development required, or it wasn't allowed to, because this is a big company and you had to go through many levels. In racing you can't wait four months for an answer. So ORECA was very instrumental in pushing that. Hugues de Chaunac's relationship with Chrysler enabled the car to be the world-beater it was."

As Viper began to rule in racing, enthusiasts wanted to share. They had the unique chance to buy the GT-2, a car that is difficult to distinguish from the GTS-R race car.

Right
To commemorate winning the FIA GT2 championship in 1997, Dodge built a run of 100 of the GT-2 racer replicas the following year. To no one's surprise, they were all sold before the first one was built.

Far right
The limited-edition GT-2 cars cost $85,200 when new and are worth significantly more than that now. A low-restriction air filter swelled the GT-2's power output to 460 horsepower and 500 foot-pounds of torque.

"I can't speak highly enough of ORECA," agreed Jim Julow, vice president of Dodge. "At what they do, they are as good as any race team on the planet. They've done a hell of a job."

Said Pierre Dieudonne, Team ORECA sporting director, "At Chrysler, we started working with a lot of dedicated and competent people. They were the team that designed and built the Viper. But of course that is a totally different world from motorsport. We had to learn working together, understanding each other's problems.

"But I think that was a very important consideration for Chrysler in their decision to go racing. They wanted to give good training to their engineers, give them the opportunity to solve different technical problems under pressure with a very short time to solve them in order to make them even better and more able to design and build and develop products for the general public in the future.

"That was the idea of their involvement in the beginning. A lot of people go racing for marketing reasons or publicity. We felt at Chrysler there was a very strong technical motivation. They wanted to stress the importance of making the engineers better at their jobs by solving problems in a very short time. For that, motor racing is the best training ground you can find."

Justin Bell shatters any illusions that Viper owners might entertain that their cars provide more than a small glimpse of the performance capabilities of the race car. "Between the road car to the race

car, it has as much similarity as a little Formula Ford car to a Formula One car," said Bell. "I'd really compare it that much. The road car is 20 percent of the race car. It is so fast, it is remarkable. Everything the road car does, the race car does so much better."

Continued Dieudonne, "We started racing the Viper in 1996, on a fairly low key. There was a lot to do at the time. We got an agreement with Chrysler to run cars. At the same time, they had another team. We did race and work together for the year '96. Then at the end of the year they made the decision to carry on only with our team. The relationship became stronger and stronger and the results got better and better.

"After one season we went from GT1 to GT2 because it was felt GT1 was getting out of control with the Porsche GT1. These cars were pure racing cars and the spirit was changing and the costs were escalating. So it was a very wise decision by Chrysler to say, 'We don't want to be involved with that; let's concentrate on the GT2 category.' Then we started winning everything. We started to dominate that category.

"The car was pretty reliable right from the beginning because it is a strong car, but there was a lot to do to make it reliably competitive. The problem that was always there was the heat dissipation. It caused all along a lot of discomfort to the drivers. You've got the big engine and the side exhaust and the big gearbox in the middle of a very confined cockpit. Therefore you have an enormous amount of heat coming into the car. And the heat coming from the brakes, especially the carbon brakes when we could use them.

The Viper GT-2 wore the same wing as the GTS-R, but alas, the street car used the more durable and way less expensive plastic bodywork, instead of the GTS-R's carbon fiber. One-piece 18-inch wheels from BBS look very much like the wheels on the race car, but they aren't exactly the same.

Some Viper buyers didn't want their cars to *look* like racers; they wanted them to *be* racers. The solution in 1999 was the Viper GTS American Club Racing (ACR) option package. Among other things, the $10,000 option deleted air conditioning, stereo, and fog lights to save weight but added the 460-horsepower engine in the GT-2.

The Viper ACR also employed the same BBS wheels used on the GT-2 and added a set of adjustable Koni shock absorbers. Unlike the professional racers, amateur ACR racers felt no need to suffer in the heat, so nearly every ACR built has the air conditioning re-added as an option.

"The heat inside the cockpit—the car is an oven if it is a hot day. The car did not suffer from that, but the drivers did. There were a lot of things we did to improve the situation, including special coating, special paint, but the problem was really always there. It went to the point that we started developing air conditioning systems for it, but we never used it because it was not fully developed.

"If a driver is destroyed, he can very easily lose two or three seconds a lap, which is a lot. Then comes a point when he is not able to go back into the car and you have to stop anyway. We always made the calculation that even if an air conditioning system would take a fair amount of power, it could be worth it.

"The biggest problem at the beginning was the gearbox," Dieudonne said. "To make it last took a little bit of time, because it is a production-based gearbox. It was in the spirit of Dodge. They wanted to improve the breed, therefore it was very important that we use components from the road car. Also there was the regulation that we had to use that gearbox. So we had to work hard to make it last."

Like poor results in the first season, unreliability of new gearboxes is another proud racing tradition, according to Bob Storck. "Obviously, the first thing that happened was the transmissions turned to junk," he said. "I don't know how many cars I've seen go through

RACING SCHOOLS

"We look on racing with a lot of pride," said Tony Estes, president of the Viper Owners Club of America. "If you go to the races, you always see a Viper corral. With Dodge sponsorship, they get us laps on the track, a place where we can park together, they give us seating together so we can come out and cheer the teams on. We look forward to the competition from the 'Vettes, because it keeps Dodge making us a better car. Dodge doesn't want to lose, Dodge doesn't like to lose, they like to see us winning."

Vipers look cool, they are fun to drive, and they sound like nothing else out there. But driving them on the street can seem like a waste of the car's potential. Where can one exercise a Viper?

The answer is a racetrack, where drivers can entertain their fantasies of miraculously saving the victory for Team Viper at Le Mans. There are a few alternatives available to Viper owners who want to try their cars on the track.

The most important thing is not to venture onto a track without experience, or if you're a novice, proper instruction. The Viper does not suffer fools gladly, and it can be an expensive lesson in driving discipline to crash from over-exuberance.

"My '96 roadster still had the '95 roadster motor, but it had the '96 coupe suspension," said Estes. "I went to the track and immediately I was four or five seconds faster [than in an original roadster]. Then my coupe came and it was about three seconds faster. It comes so well set up that just about anybody can drive it to 85 percent. But that is also the downfall to it, because at 86 percent you need to know what you are doing. At that point, if you lose it, you may be doing over 150 miles per hour. If you touch anything at 150 miles per hour, the consequences are a little bit dire."

Licensed racers need only install the required safety equipment and head to the next Sports Car Club of America race. The Viper Days Michelin Challenge series is a good option for wanna-be racers who might worry about damage to their precious toys in the competitive SCCA series. But the time, commitment, and seriousness of real racing, even at the amateur level, can be more than some people are looking for.

Viper Days, Inc., also offers lapping days with instruction for people who aren't ready yet for all-out racing, but who want to learn how to hustle their cars around the track. "They take everything from novices to experienced drivers and they put you in a group and help you improve your skills," said Estes. "I think to date they've had about 3,000 different drivers."

At the Viper Owners Invitational gatherings, there is plenty of track time for everyone, but they tend to only occur every year and a half or so.

So track days for marque clubs can also be a good chance to run the Viper hard. If the local Viper Owners Club of America chapter doesn't have anything scheduled soon, the Corvette, Porsche, and Ferrari clubs rent tracks a lot, and they are usually pretty good sports about letting people who have fun cars come play with them.

All of these possibilities assume that the driver is already in possession of a Viper. But not everyone can afford to own a Viper. Or, perhaps, a prospective Viper owner would like to see what the car is like when driven hard, and the local Dodge dealer is understandably reluctant to let him wring out the car that's on the showroom floor.

Drivers' schools are the solution. The two schools that have become best known for their use of Vipers are the Justin Bell School and the Skip Barber School. There are pros and cons to each. Probably the biggest con to the Bell school is that the Viper fleet is retiring and will be replaced by Corvettes.

Bell chose the Viper for his school because he'd made his name as a racer by winning Le Mans in a Viper. He had a long relationship with Chrysler in Europe doing promotional events, and he wanted to continue the association. "I think the Viper had such a strong cult following and image associated with it, that any of the drivers lucky enough to race for the team were identified with that product," said Bell. "I had an opportunity to start up a school. Immediately, we were able to establish ourselves as quite a force to be reckoned with, primarily off the back of the Viper."

But it was quite a challenge to teach novice racers, using a car as powerful as the Viper. "It was a lot of car, a lot of power, a lot of weight," he said. "You had people who drove Vipers who wanted to get better in their own cars, and you had people who were coming because maybe they couldn't afford one but they wanted to experience it. It was definitely a very unique car for a driving school."

Students' reactions after driving the Viper on the track fall clearly into one of two categories, Bell has observed. "Either they desperately want one, or they never want to get in one again," he said. "That is typical of a very specialist sports car. Some people are relatively intimidated by it, because on a racetrack you are going a lot quicker than you would on the road. I think people are astounded to discover the limits of the car on a racetrack, which you would never get the chance to do on the road."

The mechanics who maintained the cars were also challenged. "Because it is a big car, it is pretty heavy on tires and brakes," said Bell. "It

took us about six months to get ourselves to a very stable situation on the brakes, the disc and pad combination. Once we'd done that, it was incredibly reliable and consistent."

High engine temperatures were another issue that required sorting. "We are in south Florida, so it had a tendency to overheat a lot," said Bell. "Most cars would in 100 degree temperatures. So that was something we had to address as well. We installed an override to keep the fans going when the car is turned off, and put in bigger fans. We also ran a larger oil pan."

The antilock brakes on the 2001 and later Vipers would have been a valuable benefit for the school, said Bell. "We would've paid good money for that," he said.

The Skip Barber School lets students drive Vipers, but they are limited to autocross-style courses when driving the powerful cars. For track instruction, the more manageable Dodge Neon is the mainstay for Barber's schools. One great benefit of Barber's school is that it keeps Vipers at four tracks around the country, so students don't need to travel as far to attend as for single-location schools.

"The school originated with the BMW M3, which is a delightful car," said chief instructor Terry Earwood. "So we had to at least equal or top that when our BMW contract was up. Viper became the absolute choice."

Experiencing the Viper blows most students away, said Earwood. "I'm sure we've sold several. People go, 'Wow, I had no idea there was anything like this.'

"One of the biggest things is it is the closest thing to a race car students will ever get to drive," he continued. "It is our showcase. It makes the same statement for Barber as it does for Dodge. It says, 'We are serious about what we do.' It is the biggest attraction for our driving school, and it is a treat to share it. We have three at each location, times four locations, so we have a dozen."

To drive the Vipers, students must visit one of the school's regional bases. "Since we teach at 22 different tracks, they are too hard to transport," said Earwood.

"In our advanced driving school, we use the Viper in the autocross. Once a person has learned the proper line in a Neon, then we hop in the Viper and let them do some hot laps. Then we turn around and give them hot laps and show them what it can do."

It is the Viper's responsiveness that appeals to students the most, he said. "The minute you touch the throttle pedal, something happens. It is such a treat to drive something that responds to everything you ask it to do. Most people get out with a grin on their face."

Despite the repeated abuse by ham-fisted beginners, the school's own employees often buy them when they are sold. "They are serviced with great regularity and high quality," Earwood said. Occasionally, the cars will have a problem with the rear suspension.

"Once in a while something walks around in the rear end," Earwood said. "That is pretty rare. I don't know if an A-arm gets loose or what the problem is. The earlier cars seemed to have more trouble with that. We've had great luck with the clutches, the motors, and the transmissions. Other than the mechanics locking the keys in the car, we have no complaints."

Although the Viper has been on the road for many years, it still thrills students and attracts attention wherever it goes, he said. "It is the one car that people still follow me home when I'm driving, to ask, 'Can I look at that?'" ■

While it lasted, the Justin Bell GT Driving School USA gave students a chance to drive a Viper on the racetrack. But Bell's defection to the Corvette racing team prompted a change at his school to Chevys. *Justin Bell*

The Skip Barber racing school uses Vipers, not on the track, but on an autocross course. *Skip Barber*

development, and no engineer ever seems to think his transmission is going to have trouble, until he gets it thrown in his face."

Once sorted, the transmissions gave no trouble if they were shifted carefully. Said Dieudonne, "In those races where we needed extra drivers, some of them, if they weren't familiar with the Viper, they could damage it fairly quickly, just by the way they used it. People like Olivier Beretta, Karl Wendlinger, the regulars, they learned to use the gearbox. They could make quick gearshifts, it is not a problem; but you have to . . . [gently] apply the pressure on the lever. The car lasted through a lot of 24-hour races, so we can say it became very reliable, but it needed to be used with a little bit of care by the drivers."

As race cars are developed to become more competitive, the improvement is the result of many small upgrades, rather than a few breakthroughs. One example is the gas pedal on the race car. Driver David Donahue cited a change to the gas pedal as one of his favorite improvements to the car. On the original race car, the pedal was hinged at the top, in conventional fashion.

The ACR lacks the GT-2's gigantic rear wing, improving rear visibility, and to some eyes, appearance.

At the request of the drivers, the pedal was reconfigured to hinge at the bottom, so they could rest the heel of the foot on the floor and modulate the gas with the toes. This provided a great improvement in finesse accelerating out of bumpy curves, because the foot would be stabilized over the bumps by the heel resting on the floor, instead of bouncing in the air with the pedal, said Donahue.

"There were a few requests from the drivers, mainly for comfort," Dieudonne recalled. "It is part of those improvements and developments you can do when you are racing regularly over a period of three or four years. There must be hundreds of little examples like that, because it is constant development. Sometimes it is an engineer pointing out some detail; sometimes it is the driver doing it. All the time you can go back to the workshop or the factory and say we can make an improvement there. If not in performance, in driving comfort, and learn to make things better and better. You end up with a fantastic car."

Once the Viper achieved success, General Motors returned to sports car racing to defend the Corvette's honor. The effort went badly for the bow-tie boys for a while, but their constant improvements pushed Team Viper to keep tweaking the GTS-R.

Drivers Karl Wendlinger, Dominique Dupuy, and Olivier Beretta scored an upset overall win in the 2000 running of the 24 Hours of Daytona. At the race's start, the car is pristine.

"I think GM saw they were losing the PR battle and the Viper was romping and stomping in one of their vaunted areas of reputation," said Bob Storck. "Viper obviously kicked them in the tail and got them to go out and put their car on the table.

"I think the Corvette was a lot better, a lot quicker, because of a lot of the development the Viper had done," he said. "The Corvette is the smaller, lighter, better-balanced car. That happened at a time when the Viper folks were sitting down and making up their minds to come up with the next model.

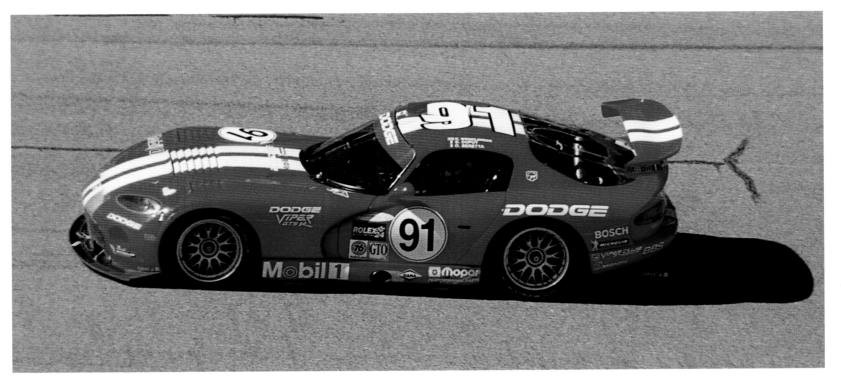

The battered and dirty but victorious Viper is still beautiful, especially to its fans.

After sweeping the top six spots at Le Mans in 1999, the Team ORECA Vipers returned to take first, second, and fourth in 2000.

Top

What does it take to win Le Mans four consecutive years? Meticulous preparation in a garage clean enough to be an operating room, maybe.

A large pile of spare parts helps to survive a hard 24 hours of racing.

"That was a good impetus for the Viper, so they didn't accept as many compromises. They went ahead and moved to a better approach, a better orientation. I think the ORECA folks got a lot more of what they asked for than if the Corvette had stayed out of the mix."

When Bob Lutz retired, he told Herb Helbig, vehicle synthesis manager for the Viper, "Above all, you've got to keep the Corvette in its place by having the Viper at the top of the performance heap. If they've got 400 horsepower, you better have more than 400 horsepower."

It was a message that was easy to hear. Said Helbig, "The biggest thing about Corvette and Viper is the Viper is still a back-to-basics car. The lure of the big horsepower, the big torque number is what the claim to fame is."

If anything improves the breed, it's competition. If the Corvette was the Viper's target, the Chevy guys were happy to finally have a home-grown competitor.

"The Corvette-Viper rivalry, we couldn't hope for a better situation," said Helbig. "Make no mistake about it, the Corvette guys are a lot like we are. We are all gearheads. They play to a little bit different audience, but they have the same kind of guys and we all have performance in mind.

"It is great to have the Viper in our competitive set because there never has really been an American sports car other than the Corvette," said Dave Hill, Corvette manager. "The Cobra was kind of an international sports car. It had some American, but some English. So the Viper certainly is the other American sports car.

"The Viper was kind of a rallying call for the whole company to show that they had courage and they had car passion," he added. "It did a huge amount for company enthusiasm. People cared passionately. You can tell it's a car that's been created by real car people, courageous people who went ahead and did something very dramatic. It certainly helped the image of the company."

A few lucky journalists who had racing experience got to drive the ORECA GTS-R during a three-day test session at France's Paul Ricard circuit in late 1996. Said Sam Moses of *AutoWeek*, "It had a humongous 650 foot-pounds of torque, which came in hard at 4,000 rpm. Drivers sometimes came off corners in a higher gear, keeping the engine under four grand when they began accelerating so they could be prepared for the blast. But I didn't find the torque to be a problem, maybe because it was drizzling that day and you had to feed the throttle gently. Surprisingly, the GTS-R had a great record racing in the wet. Hugues de Chaunac said it was because of four things: the car's weight, its excellent balance, the broad torque range, and the Michelin tires.

Crews must also survive the night, pitting the cars at regular intervals, with crashes and mechanical failures demanding extra attention.

While the rear wing gets the aerodynamic headlines, the rear undertray and front splitter (the black "chin" on this car) toil in anonymity. But they are critical components, and the 2003 Viper gets a fully enclosed smooth bottom for ground effects.

For a season and a half in 1999 and 2000, Vipers had their way with the archrival Corvette team. But the yellow menace loomed ever larger in the Viper's mirrors and finally snatched victory from the Vipers midway through the 2000 season. Viper partisans would point out that the 'Vettes were using much larger displacement engines than are available in street Corvettes.

"The engine was amazingly smooth—it felt smoother than the GTS road car. Borla stainless-steel headers exited behind the doors, and the howl from the exhaust was more like what you would expect from a V-10, unlike the understated rasp of the GTS.

"I was impressed with how smoothly the Borg-Warner six-speed shifted. Some of the drivers complained about the long throw of the lever, but as Olivier Beretta said, 'It's fine if you're affirmative,'" Moses continued. "And I'd never driven a car that had a more responsive throttle action during downshift blips, thanks to a light flywheel inside a magnesium bellhousing. The engine zing was so wonderfully sharp and sweet-sounding that I wished I could drop from sixth to second gear for every turn, just to play with the gearbox.

"At Daytona, David Donohue had described the handling as 'floaty,' but it felt pretty neutral to me—and to Beretta, later, when he drove with me in the passenger seat taking mental notes. The power-assist rack-and-pinion steering is taken off the road car, with solid bushings replacing rubber. It wasn't especially light to the touch, but the car felt light in weight. It also felt large, thanks to those big bulbous fenders framing the sides of the long hood.

"It was a pretty memorable day, blasting down the backstraight in the drizzle, reaching 167 miles per hour in sixth gear."

"I'm glad that racing was pursued with vigor," said proud Viper papa Bob Lutz. "It was already getting very promising when I was still at Chrysler. The big Le Mans success and the outright win at Daytona, that's just wonderful. The ORECA team [has] just done a fabulous job with the car. I just

wish it got more coverage, and I wish we made more of it. The otherwise outstanding Chrysler PR team [winning Le Mans], went completely over their heads. They just didn't do anything with it."

For fans, the question is where the Viper goes from here, since Dodge has ended its factory involvement in sports car racing to concentrate on stock cars and because the new-generation Viper is available, initially at least, only in roadster form.

"With the privateers, the Viper will still be a very, very strong racing car for some years to come," said Dieudonne. "But once you stop development, age comes quite quickly in motorsport. I would say the car is mature now. How long does it take to go from mature to old? That is the question. Also, the private teams don't have the resources or the knowledge or the experience we have, so the chances of them winning against a factory team like the Corvette are very small."

Playstation sponsorship for Team ORECA's racing program was a good match. Most kids' exposure to the Viper comes from piloting the car in video games, such as "Viper Racing" from Sierra Sports.

Another race (in this case the 2000 Sonoma Grand Prix in the American Le Mans Series) and another Viper sweep of the podium.

The next generation of Viper owners might be introduced to the car through video racing games such as "Viper Racing." It was no surprise to see Playstation appear as the primary sponsor of Team ORECA because of the popularity of the game. Sierra Sports is particularly proud of the realistic damage to crashed cars in its game, a feature that Team ORECA's drivers would probably like to be able to turn off. *Sierra Sports*

But the image-making machine had achieved its goal.

"The fact that Viper was a competitive race car has always had a major influence over Team Viper," said Jim Julow. "When we came back to the States with the American Le Mans Series is when it really invaded the owner psyche. We announced it to them and there was widespread euphoria. It is just one other piece of bragging rights it brings to their vehicle that validates it as really the true race car for the street. If it wasn't validated with the performance of the vehicle itself, this adds that final level. It's important to these guys to know that they have got the best that they can buy.

"There is no question racing has helped loyalty," he continued. "It has also helped sell to people who have come out of other fairly exotic sports cars. I'm not the 'Win on Sunday, sell on Monday' person, but I think there is a credibility and validation, particularly for the person who looks for a Dodge-type product. I think the motorsports activities have an impact on that level. It gives you a substance that was missing. There are certain thresholds for being a substantial, successful, mainstream domestic brand. I think this was part of it."

Only by competing against and beating the likes of Porsche, could Viper expect to build the reputation it wanted. "We don't want to be as narrow as Porsche," said Julow. "We've got to have cars, we've got to have trucks, and we've got to have minivans. But we see more interest in performance-type models, which I think is a result of the racing success."

To think that Dodge would be a serious competitor of Porsche seemed absurd not long ago. Today the Viper is respected in Europe. "The design philosophy, the execution of the car, the personality of the car is today a huge asset," said Francois Castaing. "The car is becoming a cult in a way, with a fan club and owners club. It has raced and won Le Mans, which just added to the reputation of the car. The Europeans were kind of skeptical about the car early on because they thought the car was overly simplistic and not sophisticated enough. But if you look at what is going on, the Viper is becoming what Porsche was a few years ago at Le Mans."

When Dodge introduced its GTS-R race version of the Viper in 1996, it was to widespread skepticism. Now the car is recognized as a champion in international sports car racing. It's not just a muscle-bound American hot rod anymore.

The shape is familiar, and Tommy Archer's name is still on the roof, but this Viper is a whole new beast. This is its first year of competition in the Sports Car Club of America Trans-Am series. The Viper looks similar to the Le Mans Vipers, but it's actually powered by a V-8 engine, at least until an equivalency formula can be devised to handicap the V-10 so that other cars can remain competitive. *Cinjo Racing*

VIPERMANIA

Nearly every car with any kind of character at all has a following of enthusiastic owners. For some of them, there is little explanation for the attraction. There are clubs for Daihatsu cars that have Internet Web sites, for example. Some clubs are more like support groups than enthusiast groups; old cars with hard-to-find parts that require specific repair knowledge often spawn these kinds of clubs. People tend to be attracted by the challenge of keeping their quirky or unusual car running.

But the attraction of the Viper is clear. Viper owners positively love their cars and like to hang out with others who feel the same way. They love to modify and customize their cars, and so they like to visit with people who can appreciate the changes they've made and who have ideas of their own. Even outside the clubs, the Viper has attracted a following, from kids who have Viper posters and video games to adults who felt an irresistible attraction the first time they laid eyes on a Viper.

Viper owners gather their cars at regional meetings all over the country, at regular events like this car show.

"Viper owners are a really interesting group of people," said Tony Estes, who should know. He's president of the Viper Owners Club of America. "They come from all walks of life, but one thing they have in common is an appreciation for an American sports car and a powerful sports car. That's what you get with a Viper. Owning a Viper is like owning your own roller coaster, only you don't have to wait in line for the ride.

"Even now, in the eighth year of production, there are only 11 or 12 thousand of them ever made," he continued. "So there is the mystique of having something that is rare. I had always wanted a musclecar when I was growing up but didn't have the money for it. When I looked at the Viper for the first time, I fell in love with the car and ordered one.

"A real Cobra is about $500,000, so I wasn't in the market for a Cobra. I've raced the Porsches; I've raced the Corvettes. To be honest, there is just not any comparison. With the Porsche Turbo, you're always waiting for the turbo to spool up. The Corvette seems sedate compared to the

Francois Castaing and Bob Lutz (left to right) survey what they have wrought, standing in a sea of Vipers at the first Viper Owners Invitational event. *John Lamm*

Viper. It doesn't handle nearly as well; it won't corner as quickly. For an everyday car to use on the street, it may be OK. But the Viper is something you can drive to the track, race it all day, and then drive it home."

The opinion of a fanatic, perhaps, but that might describe most Viper owners.

"Viper owners are the core of the Dodge-owner body," said Jim Julow, president of Dodge. "They were some of the first converts when the new Dodge started out a few years ago. They are the most passionate of our owner groups.

"In 1992–93, there were people who would take [the word] *Dodge* off anything they bought. It was a *Viper* they bought, not a *Dodge* Viper. Now you see them putting *Dodge* back on the car. I'm extremely impressed with the level of brand loyalty these folks express."

"I owned a Dodge truck 20 years ago," said Estes. "It would run forever, but the body parts literally fell off. The door hinges broke; it was a *Sanford and Son* sort of thing. I went into the dealer to order my Viper and saw the new Dodge Ram. While we were there we saw the Jeep Grand Cherokee, and my wife liked it and we bought one of those. I liked her Jeep, so we bought another one. The original Viper purchase ended up with seven Vipers, 11 trucks, three Neons, four Jeep Grand Cherokee Limiteds, and a new minivan. I went from a Chevy man to a Dodge man in a heartbeat."

Dodge quickly recognized the value of cultivating such enthusiasm among Viper fans, so in 1994 the company organized a tour of the factory, in what became the first of many Viper Owners Invitational events. Now part of the Viper legend, owners point to the VOIs when explaining their loyalty.

"Where else do you see the president . . . marketing, design, suspension . . . [T]hey are all there," said Estes. "You can walk up to the president of Dodge, shake his hand and tell him what you think, and two years later it will be on the car. It is amazing that they actually listen to what you said. What other car company rents a track for a week, hires instructors to sit in the car with

Continued on next page

There are many activities at the track other than just lapping the road course. This autocross course allows drivers to practice their finesse, rather than their bravery. DaimlerChrysler also provided its Neon ACR club racing cars for this exercise.

you, gives you four different venues to drive in, and then says 'Thank you for coming?' "

The Viper Owners Invitational tradition started with that relatively humble plant tour in July 1994. The second event was also relatively small, held at the Monterey Historic Races and Pebble Beach Concours in August 1995, where Dodge introduced the GTS Coupe. On Memorial Day 1996, the company held VOI.3 (the abbreviation for Invitationals is VOI.1, VOI.2, and so on) at the Indianapolis Motor Speedway, where the new coupe served as the pace car. After 1996, VOI began to transform into the massive event it is today, complete with racetrack sessions, driver training, and tours through the local countryside.

"This is probably one of the best customer relationship marketing programs in the industry," said Bob Champine, senior manager of Dodge Marketing Plans. "No other car company in the industry, I believe, does things like this. The benefit to us is trying to nurture a relationship, trying to reward them for purchasing our products. The Dodge Viper folks have been extremely good to us in purchasing our other products as a result of the Viper experience. We bring them into the fold. We give them a great experience.

"We have a similar program over on the Jeep side, with the Jeep Jamborees and Jeep 101 events, which is a little bit of driving experience, a great social weekend. They do those programs five, six, seven times a year, but they don't have the numbers of people in one location that I do with our program. We've had people come from all over the world: Switzerland, Germany, England, Japan.

"I've got some of the most enthusiastic customers I've ever seen in my life," Champine continued. "We have folks who have converted their dining rooms into garages. You know, some of the collections these people have are just unbelievable. The Viper memorabilia they collect and the amount of money that they spend on this stuff. The vacations they take, the club activities, the charities they support with the vehicle."

The tales that are told by Viper owners at these events reveal their spirit. "We had one owner go off a cliff when he did a downshift," said Champine. "Somebody that totals their vehicle and

Viper owners also love any chance to blast their cars down a drag strip. The Invitationals in Las Vegas and St. Louis both had drag strips at the same location as the road race track, helping centralize activities.

Viper fans can't spend the whole time inside their cars, so Dodge tries to locate the Invitationals in cities that have other attractions and activities. While the arch is the best-known landmark in St. Louis, owners seemed to prefer attending the parties in Laclede's Landing, the riverfront social district.

blacks out in the process, and the first thing they say when they come to is, 'Thank god we're alive; now let's hop a plane because we've got a party to go to,' rather than going home and crying in your beer. And at the Las Vegas Viper Owners Invitational we had someone who was stopped by the locals on the way. They road-blocked him, because they couldn't stop him at 140 miles per hour. He never made the event."

The upgraded VOI made its debut in Orlando in July 1997. Orlando was chosen not only for the Disney hotels but for its proximity to a drag strip and to the Sebring racetrack, not to mention other famous attractions in the vicinity. "It was just the one big, most expensive party we've held, to the tune of about 800 people," said Champine.

It took a little while for Dodge's budget to recover from the Orlando bash, so VOI.6 waited until April 1999. It was held in Las Vegas, because like Orlando, it had local attractions, a racetrack, and the hotel capacity to handle a crowd.

"We had 2,000 people and 800 cars, so Las Vegas was our biggest event so far," said Champine. "Unless we go back to Las Vegas, we probably won't plan one to that magnitude again. We had the full venue of track activity at Las Vegas Motor Speedway, where we did autocross, drag strip, and road course. We actually brought in a number of our four-wheel-drive Dodge products and, off on one spot of speedway grounds, had the ability on the motorcycle course to do a four-wheel-drive driving exercise, driving over the moguls and hills. That was really an exciting activity. Our president at that time, Tom Stallkamp, spent the majority of his weekend over in the four-by-four stuff, while Tom Gale and others spent a lot of their time on the various venues that were central to the track."

For the next gathering, in August 2000, Dodge rallied the troops in St. Louis. The city might have lacked the flash of Las Vegas, but it had a new racetrack located only minutes from downtown. Said Champine, "We blew them away with the exercise we gave them in St. Louis. Everybody got as much track time as they could handle."

More than 1,100 of the faithful arrived in about 600 Vipers. They came from 44 states, as well as Canada, Germany, Japan, New Zealand, and the United Kingdom. The combined Vipers totaled 275,000 horsepower and would have stretched in a line for more than a mile and a half. The 3,000 laps driven around the racetrack totaled 3,750 miles at racing speed.

VOI.7 will be in Detroit in 2002. Like the earliest events, this Invitational will coincide with a new car. Some lucky customers will actually take delivery of their 2003 Vipers at the event, so that excitement may render other activities superfluous. Until next time, at least. ■

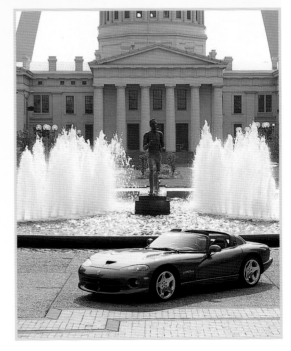

CHAPTER EIGHT

VIPER 3.0:VGX

The Viper GTS/R concept car, which debuted at the 2000 North American International Auto Show, was the first public hint of Team Viper's design plans for the next-generation Viper. Unfortunately, the company hasn't yet confirmed plans for a coupe to be produced.

John Lamm

When Team Viper developed the new chassis, suspension, and engine for the 1996 Viper, there was no question that they were giving customers exactly what they wanted: more power, better handling, and less weight. And it all came in two great packages: a gorgeous coupe and a roadster that was only slightly changed in appearance. But the 1996 and later cars were still based on the flawed 1992 RT/10, which was now getting old by any standards. The worst thing that could happen to the Viper would be for it to lose its spot at the top of the performance heap. That was its *raison d'etre*.

But fending off Porsche, Ferrari, Corvette, Lamborghini, Aston-Martin, Jaguar, and more, couldn't be done with half-hearted tweaks. It was time for a new car. So the debate was launched over what an all-new Viper, the Viper for the 21st century, should be.

"We are going to keep our place in the queue; if that means 500 horsepower and 500 foot-pounds of torque, then that's what it will be," argued Tom Gale. "If it means that we've got to do things that will give it the capability of being the benchmark in terms of slalom, if it means we've got to keep it at the top of the heap in braking, if it means all of those things, then that's what we'll do.

"There will be a lot of areas of refinement that I think would be expected," he added. "We've already come a long way. You can see the levels of refinement from those early cars to where we are now, even. It is dramatic. The car is just incredible and just awesome."

The new Viper was code-named VGX early in its development. "In 1997, we started to look conceptually at the next-generation Viper and what we wanted it to be," said John Fernandez, executive engineer of Specialty Vehicle Engineering. "We spent about six months trying to figure out where we wanted to go with the car. We knew that in the time frame we were talking about bringing it out, that the old car would be 10 years old. That is really old for a car. Most of the time it's three or four years."

The issue was whether qualitative improvements—refinements—would spoil the Viper's elemental nature. "In these early discussions, everything was on the table," said Fernandez. "Aspects of the Viper, which many enthusiasts consider essential 'Viperness,' we examined and reaffirmed. We talked about a lot of things, such as whether we wanted to perpetuate the Viper as it was, with the V-10, or whether we wanted to go a completely different route with the VGX. But when everything was said and done, we decided the car was an icon unto itself and to the Dodge brand. So we decided we wanted to make it an evolution of the car, rather than a complete revolution, in terms of its image.

"We wanted to continue to keep the car in the price range we'd been able to bring the car out in," he added. "We wanted to stay in the $85K price range. We didn't want to jump to the $300,000 price range. And if you look at what we got, from a performance standpoint, the speeds we are capable of doing, the kinds of g-loadings we are capable of pulling in the turns, the VGX is capable of playing with a $300,000 car. You can buy it for less than a hundred thousand bucks."

"The engineering is true to the original plan and is excellent," said Roy Sjoberg. "Our base mission, as I established it, was 0-100-0 miles per hour. Do whatever you have to to set a new 0-100-0 record. I believe the VGX will set a new level for that criteria."

The fierce-looking GTS/R concept took its design cues directly from the GTS-R race car. The concept featured a pumped-up 500-horsepower engine and 10-spoke alloy wheels, accurately forecasting the same features on the 2003 Viper.

The stronger engine, lightweight carbon-fiber bodywork, and even bigger 14-inch brakes pushed the GTS/R's performance to new levels: 0 to 60 miles per hour in 3.8 seconds, quarter-mile in 11.8 seconds, and a 200-mile-per-hour top speed. In the all-important 0-100-0 Viper benchmark, the time was trimmed to just 13.2 seconds. *John Lamm*

DaimlerChrysler first revealed plans for the 2003 Viper when it displayed the Viper GTS/R Race Car Concept at the 2000 North American International Auto Show in Detroit. Designed by Osam Shikado, that car was a coupe, outfitted with a fuel cell, racing harnesses, and aerodynamic features for racing. One year later, the 2003 Viper RT-10 convertible production car made its debut at the Detroit show. Shikado stayed true to the unmistakable Viper lines of the concept. "But the new one is more sophisticated," he said. "I used more crisp lines on the fender, the top of the body sides, and also the side gill."

The new car's designation has changed slightly, as the RT/10 becomes the 2003 RT-10 in showrooms by summer 2002. A new Viper emblem faces viewers straight on, with a more confrontational stance, completing the badging changes. The RT-10 is also a true convertible. "The integral convertible top is going to make current Viper owners jealous," said Brian Cojocari, Viper program manager. "It makes it an all-weather car," he said.

While the carbon-fiber and brushed-aluminum materials did not make the transition to the production model, the GTS/R's dash design and gauge layout is almost unchanged in the 2003 Viper. Sadly, the cool throttle plate–style air vents didn't make the cut.

The GTS/R's rooftop air duct is derived from the air intakes on the Viper racing cars. We can only wait for a new-generation coupe to learn whether the duct will be used in street trim. *John Lamm*

Where the original car was a targa, with a fixed-roof structure behind the occupants, the RT-10 is smooth from the cockpit to the taillights. And where the original Viper's roof panel required bending, folding, and mutilating to fit in the trunk, the new car's top folds down easily, like any good convertible. It's manual, so there are no electric motors adding weight to the car, and it has a convenient central latch on the windshield header. Its rear window is glass, with an embedded defroster.

The section of the top directly over the occupants' heads is rigid, so the car will be more quiet and comfortable inside. All possible applications were considered for this part, including testing its ability to support the weight of a person seated on it during a parade. "We affectionately refer to this test as the beauty queen test," said Cojocari.

Occupant comfort, which merited virtually no consideration on the original RT/10, was a priority on the RT-10, said Fernandez. "We looked at [improved] passenger compartment cooling, how we distributed the air in the car. That was always problematic, and we wanted to improve the interior package [ergonomics] of the car. In the old car, the driver does not sit absolutely perpendicular to the wheel; he's in there at kind of an angle. And the steering wheel is at an angle to the car itself. It is not square to the world."

Viper owners approved of the results. "The interior of the new car is very much superior," said Steve Ferguson, founding member of the Viper Owners Club of America. "You can tell they listened to us.

This view of the GTS/R emphasizes the car's slab-sided styling, which is very beneficial on the racetrack, even if it meets with mixed reviews from fans. *John Lamm*

Drilled aluminum pedals in the show car may not have made it into production, but they sure looked good. There is always the aftermarket for such custom touches. *John Lamm*

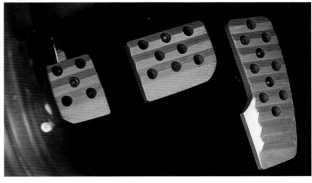

The gauges and controls are right where you can see them. It will be much more user-friendly, but not so user-friendly that it's a high-horsepower Corvette."

"Design-wise, it's a mixed bag," said Roy Sjoberg. "I think you will get a different customer with that styling, more of a Corvette customer than the original Viper owner. It is certainly true to the Viper general looks, and it is a very pleasant evolution; but it is not bodacious, which the original Viper was."

"I think the styling has become what I like to refer to as 'sanitized for your protection,'" said Bob Lutz. "I don't think it has the boldness, and the presence and the uniqueness of the original Viper and Viper GTS. I'm sure it's a phenomenal car and I'm sure it's a world-beater, so I can easily put my aesthetic reservations on hold. I very much like what I hear about the car in terms of its improved dynamics, lower weight, higher power, new chassis, greater torsional and beam stiffness, and so forth. I am absolutely convinced that it is a much better car and it is going to be successful."

Said John Fernandez, "The big thing we did when we began to design the new Viper was we sat down and wrote what we called a mission document, which contained all of the things that we felt we wanted to improve on the old car. We wanted to improve the handling. The skid pad numbers that you got on the old Viper were good numbers, but what we wanted to improve was what I call the 'progressivity' of the car. We wanted the car to be more progressive in terms of what it did when it made transitions.

"So we worked very hard on the geometry of the car. We modified the suspension pickup points to improve the antidive and antisquat characteristics. We improved the toe curves on the car. And we worked very closely with Michelin to develop a brand-new tire for the car that we feel is something way beyond where we were with the old tire. Not just the size of the tire; we've come up with a whole new construction and new compounds for the tire."

Team Viper also worked very hard on the frame. "In the low-volume application, for most of the cars in this neighborhood, the architecture is pretty much the same," Fernandez said. "The issue becomes, do you get completely exotic and go with completely aluminum castings and things like that?"

The answer for VGX was no, mostly to keep the price down. Still, the new frame is dramatically more rigid than the old. "Percentage-wise, we're double the characteristics of what we have today in the roadster, and it approaches what you would get in the coupe," said Fernandez.

Next page
Once unveiled, it was obvious that the GTS/R had been a good indication of the design team's philosophy for the new car. Though it is a convertible, and lacks the racing theme of the GTS/R, the 2003 Viper is clearly a continuation of that theme. *John Lamm*

The original Viper attained much of its rigidity from large amounts of steel. The new Viper got the rigidity without the mass.

"We looked at a number of different cars [for comparison]," Fernandez said. "We looked at the Honda S2000. We took a hard look at the Lotus Elise, because of its use of aluminum and the way they laid that car out. We did use some of the conceptual ideas in that car. We didn't necessarily use the same materials that they used, but some of the concepts that they had. The Audi A8 was another one we took a hard look at because it had some superior numbers with the types of materials we were looking at.

"The basic architecture of the car is not much different than the original car," he continued. "But we spent a lot of time looking at materials. We've got some carbon-fiber usage on this car that we didn't have on the original, and [we] have gone further than ever before on the use of magnesium in the components. Virtually every panel is made differently. And our carbon-fiber use has not been for cosmetics. It's been for gaining structure at a reduced weight. I'm not at liberty to tell you exactly where it is used yet. In magnesium, we've got the biggest piece of magnesium that the industry has yet to see. In that one piece, we saved 28 pounds versus what we were doing in the old car. It's a part of the frame; that's about all I can tell you.

"We kept working that, taking weight out here and putting different materials in there, to the point we got not only the weight we were looking for but the torsional rigidity and bending rigidity we were looking for. What allowed us to do that was we spent much more time in modeling the car. We designed the car, we then modeled the car, we redesigned the car, we ran it through the model again, redesigned it again. This is one thing Roy Sjoberg didn't have that I took advantage of. We have a whole crew here in the SVE group that does our modeling. I've got some of the best modelers in the company.

"The other thing that has been helping us a lot on the car is, that, through the merger, we got access to the research centers in Germany that Mercedes-Benz had. We've got about 1,500 people who work in research in Munich and Ulm and Stuttgart. We've got access to those groups; we've spent a lot of time over there. For the VGX, we've got about three or four projects that we've been working with them."

The 2003 Viper is about 125 pounds lighter than the old one, despite its longer wheelbase, increased width, and bigger wheels and tires, whose size would have been unimaginable just a few years ago. The 18x10-inch front wheels wear P275/35ZR18 Michelins; the rear wheels are 19x13 inches, fitted with P345/30ZR19 tires that would look at home on an Indy car.

The new Viper is 175.5 inches in total length, about an inch shorter than the outgoing car. But it adds nearly 10 inches in width to an already wide car, growing to 84.8 inches from door handle to door handle. The wheelbase is stretched a couple of inches, to 98.8 inches, for better stability, while the front and rear track remain almost unchanged. The final result is an expected curb weight of 3,357 pounds.

Like economist Adam Smith's famous hidden hand, Carroll Shelby's far-reaching influence continued to steer the Viper's development. "I worked for Carroll Shelby for five years, and I learned a lot of things from him," Fernandez said. "One thing that Carroll taught me was that when you are looking at high performance, the first thing you look at is weight.

"His rationale is this: When you're at the limit of adhesion in a corner with a car, it doesn't make any difference if you've got an extra hundred horsepower or an extra thousand horsepower, the car

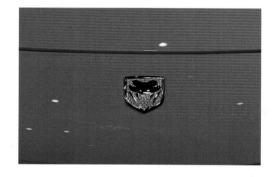

Top
A small change in the name is shown on the fender. The new car is the RT-10 instead of the RT/10. As if having GTS, GTS/R, GT-2, and GTS-R concept cars didn't introduce enough potential for confusion. Also, Team ORECA's racing cars wore the logo GTSR/T on their fenders.

The new emblem on the hood presents a meaner-looking snake that glares straight ahead, in place of the original smirking snake design.

The biggest break from the past is the use of a true convertible top in place of the RT/10's targa roof. The rigid panel over the cockpit, insulated fabric, and glass back window make the new Viper a true all-weather convertible. *John Lamm*

won't go around that corner any faster. What you need is less weight or a bigger radius. Carroll always put at the top of his list: weight, then horsepower, then cooling. I never forgot that lesson."

With the frame, suspension, and tires all upgraded, the last chassis component to address was the brake system. This had been a contentious issue for the original Viper, and that debate spilled over to the VXG. "We took a real hard look at where we thought the rest of the performance world was going, because we wanted the new car to still be the king of the hill," said Fernandez. "The biggest area we thought needed improvement was the brakes. We needed to improve the complete

Corvette owners, get used to this view! Attention to underbody airflow is suggested by the Viper's nonfunctional rear diffuser exits under the bumper. Perhaps, like the fog lamp openings that can be converted to brake ducts, these openings will be made functional in future racing versions.

A center latch on the windshield header is standard on expensive sports cars these days, so the Viper has a single handle to release the roof.

The manually operated roof folds back and settles down into the boot without flipping upside down, in the manner of the Porsche 911 Cabriolet. That makes a boot cover unnecessary, because the smooth outer roof provides an attractive appearance.

Once folded into its well, the convertible top doesn't intrude on the Viper's generous trunk space.

brake system of the car. Anytime there was a run-off between us and anyone else, we always got killed on the braking side. That was primarily due to everybody else having ABS.

"We had a big debate about that. We said 'Jeez, is this the right thing to do for the car? Is ABS with electronics the kind of image we want?' When the original car was done, it certainly wasn't the right way to go. It wasn't part of the image. For the new car, we said, 'This is where it's at.' It isn't like we're ruining the image of the car. This car is still a back-to-basics car, but 'basics' in today's world includes ABS. If you want to play, you better be there. That's how we rationalized that, but it was a long, drawn-out debate on that."

With a new foundation in place, Team Viper was ready to give owners what they seem to want most: more power. Comedian/actor Tim Allen may race Fords, but the Viper is certainly the automotive epitome of his "masculinist" philosophy of "more power!"

"We wanted to make sure we stayed on top in terms of the performance of the V-10," Fernandez said. "We're talking about 500-plus horsepower range and 500-plus foot-pounds of torque. Going along with that, we now have 505 cubic inches, in terms of displacement of the engine."

Neither the seats nor the steering wheel were square to the rest of the car on the original Viper. The 2003 Viper improves ergonomics by correcting those problems.

The new engine has been dubbed "DVX" by some familiar with its development, because DVX is the Roman numeral for 505. The nickname also recalls the legendary Ford Cosworth DFV engine that dominated Formula One and (in turbocharged form) Indy car racing for decades.

The Viper's old engine was a meager 488 cubic inches. The metric measure has grown from 8.0 liters to 8.3. Power and torque are rated at improbably round numbers of 500 each, making the engine 500 inches (sort of), 500 horsepower, and 500 foot-pounds of torque. Some of these numbers surely vary a bit, but it makes for better ad copy at an even 500.

"Obviously we wanted to stay with a V-10," said Fernandez. "There wasn't much of a debate around the engine. The idea of having the V-10 has become part of the mystique of the Viper. There were some things we wanted to improve on the engine. We wanted to improve the NVH characteristics. We wanted to improve the total reliability/durability package, especially in very heavy-duty use.

"I don't think, when the team originally did the engine, they had any idea how many people were going to be out there racing these things. So we spent a lot of time looking at our notes from our GTS-R program in the world championship cars, what we did with those motors. We were very reliable, having won Le Mans three times, and Daytona and Sebring, and a lot of 24-hour races. So we had a lot that we grafted onto the new engine from what we learned from our motorsports experience in the GTS-R program.

"It was the intake side of the engine that we wanted to improve. Today we have twin throttle bodies. In the future, we're going to be going away from that because we can tune the engine a lot better with a single-staged type of throttle body. The intake side of the equation is completely new.

A top that stows completely out of the way, better air conditioning, and more comfortable seats could make the Viper a supreme top-down cruising machine.

Most of what it improves on, we found with the GTS-R program. When you see the intake manifold, if you look at a GTS-R, you'll see similarities there.

"We didn't change the basic internals of the engine other than the dimensions. The bore and stroke have changed. The combustion chamber is the same as we are using today. The basic fundamentals of the engine we have today are an evolution of the current engine. Where the improvements have come from are things we have learned from our motorsports activities. Primarily in the ability to improve the efficiency of the engine, the volumetric efficiency in the intake side of it, and the exhaust side.

"We also wanted to improve the cooling of the engine. The old car, when you'd get into really hot situations, was always right there at the ragged edge. So we wanted to make sure we improved that."

VGX designers knew they needed aggressive styling, but they also had to have a body that used the wind to best advantage. The wind tunnel doesn't appreciate the beauty of flowing curves, so they are largely absent from the VGX.

"We wanted to spend a lot more time in aerodynamic analysis of the car," Fernandez said. "The original car spent a lot of time trying to stay true to the styling exercise that was shown at the North American Auto Show in 1989. In order to do that, we made some aerodynamic compromises.

"This time, we hadn't showed any car, so we knew [we] could go to the wind tunnel with the design exercises Tom Gale and his guys were working on. We spent a tremendous amount of time in the wind tunnel, to make sure that we got the maximum amount of leverage from the style of the body. And we've gone to a flat-bottomed car, with a full belly pan.

"The front of our car today, every little detail in the grille openings to the radiuses we're using on the fascias and each edge, was work that we did in the wind tunnel. Every little piece of air we get going into the thing is purposeful, to cool the brakes, to cool the engine, and to get air into the intake system. We spent a lot of time on the front end of the car. When you haven't shown the car to the general public, and you are working with the design office on a cooperative basis, we were able to do a lot more with this car than the guys were with the first car, because they already had it out there.

The racing influence on the 2003 Viper RT-10 is subtle but pervasive. Hidden alongside the heater controls is the new Viper's bright red starter button, just like the push-button starter on the race cars.

One interior change that could cause some angst about the Viper's intent is the arrival of a cupholder. But hey, Chrysler is the "minivan company."

The 8.3-liter engine at the other end of that starter button is still under wraps, but like this Corvette engine, it will feature a single large throttle body in place of the dual throttle bodies used on earlier cars. The change improves the precision of throttle control. *General Motors Corporation*

The original Viper's clamshell hood with integrated front fenders is gone, replaced by a conventional hood and fenders that give owners easier access to the engine bay and are easier for the assembly plant to install.

Elegant clear wraparound taillight lenses with flush-mounted backup lights are the style of the day, and the new Viper wears them well.

"We feel that this car is aerodynamically superior to anything out there on the road today. That's not in terms of drag coefficient, because when you've got the kind of horsepower we've got, the speeds that we've got, what becomes more and more important than just the coefficient of drag number is aerodynamic balance of the car. As an example, a Formula One car has a terrible coefficient of drag number, but the aerodynamic balance and the downforce you can generate on an F1 car is just awesome. That is what we were looking for."

Perhaps anticipating some resistance to the sleeker, less voluptuous styling, a bit of effort and expense went into something that was purely aesthetic but would return the car to its original configuration: side pipes. The side pipes were an important styling cue on the original concept car that helped link the car to the Cobras that inspired it. The pipes stayed on the car when it went into production, almost as if to say, "We told you so," to skeptics who were sure the car would be disappointingly watered-down in production form.

"It is a neat thing," said Sjoberg. "It is not at all a vital thing, it's just neat to have side exhaust. It looks cool and you have a different sound because you're hearing five cylinders, not 10 cylinders."

Dodge had dropped the side pipes in favor of rear exhaust because of the impossibility of meeting new EPA OBD II requirements with side pipes. But technology marches forward, and the 2003 side pipes could pass the tests. So designers who let the wind tunnel make some of the styling decisions had a way to link the new car with its forebear.

"We had to do some technical wizardry there to make sure we didn't get into high back pressures," said Fernandez. "With the electronic noise attenuator system, they've been able to

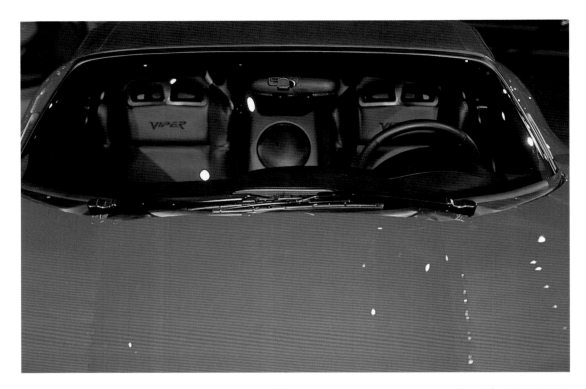

The unconventional windshield wipers are another trademark feature that fans expect to see, so the Viper RT-10 continues with the same type.

Massive 19-inch rear wheels are a step forward for the Viper. The new 10-spoke design mimics the appearance of the wheels on the race cars. All-new Michelins, designed just for the Viper, will be mounted on the new cars when they arrive in showrooms.

put the muffler back in the exhaust, but much less restrictive, allowing rapid airflow. You don't need the restriction to get the noise correction, you are doing that electronically. And NGK now has a sensor that can take both heat and moisture [in a side exhaust environment].

"Electronic noise cancellation is a technology the corporation was interested in," Fernandez said. "Part of our charter as the SVE group is to develop technologies so that other platforms can use them. In this case, there were a couple [of] platforms that were very interested in the technology of noise cancellation and the ability to tune things using the noise cancellation technology. So we have applied that on our car."

The redesign also gave Team Viper an opportunity to make the Viper easier to manufacture. While the company wanted to continue with a hand-assembled, low-volume car, eliminating some production bottlenecks could simultaneously improve quality and make it easier to meet demand for the cars.

"We wanted to make some processing improvements," Fernandez said. "At the Conner Avenue Assembly Plant today, we pride ourselves on crafting the car. And we want to be still crafting the car, but we want to get to be a little more in terms of Henry Ford's assembly-line mass-production line on the car.

"On one side, we are trying to craft a car here. It is a low-volume car; we're going to make between eight and 13 a day. But on the other side, you want quality levels commensurate with the best cars out there today, and some of what you do in crafting a car, in contrast to mass-produce a car, is a little bit in conflict with that. We spent a lot of time on, 'What do we want to craft and what do we want to mass-produce here?' "

In preparation for manufacturing the new car, prototypes are under construction to test the new ideas. This will let the company attend to the final details that make the difference between a good car and a great one.

"Today, we are finishing up building our first program-level cars, which are in fact skinned prototypes," he said. "These cars look exactly like the cars we are going to go into production with. They have all the pieces and designs, but they are not necessarily off production tools yet. Next year is our big year for the development phase of the project. I really think this is what is going to bring this car off: the refinement and attention to detail.

"That is what I have been pushing the guys on. I've been saying, we are 95 percent of the way there, we've got the car that we want, we've got the pieces that we want, we've got the components, we've got the systems. But, guys, we've got to work on the 2 percent solution, that last little attention to detail. The fit and finish of the body panels. The tuning of suspension, to make sure it is just the way we want it. The calibration of engine, to make sure we've got that just the way we want it."

The big question for Viper fans is whether or not there will be a coupe. The company originally planned to do a coupe along with the convertible, but the VGX program couldn't command the money and people. "We took a look at doing both versions at the same time, but we just couldn't do it," said Cojocari.

In addition to buyers who might prefer the coupe's styling, the better aerodynamics of a coupe are needed if the factory is to return to sports car racing. So perhaps the desire for a racing car will lead to production of a new Viper coupe.

Next page
Top down, the new Viper retains its rakish styling, with a line running almost straight back from the top of the windshield, through the roll hoops to the tail. *John Lamm*

The louvered vents for the engine bay have moved off the fenders and onto the hood, looking a bit more like the Jaguar E–type vents that inspired them.

"I've got about 120 guys who work over here and there's not a guy out here who doesn't want to have our race program again," said Fernandez. "If we go back to racing, and we all want to do that, we want to go back and be as successful as before. We want to go back and dominate. In order to do that, we need an all-new car. And I would agree that all-new car probably needs to have a roof on it."

The racing program is wildly popular with Viper owners, and the transfer of technology from the race car to the street car has been a tremendous success. There's a good chance the factory Vipers will return to Le Mans and Daytona, especially since the factory-backed Corvette has taken over as king of the GT class, with its own overall victory at Daytona in 2001.

Team ORECA would likely play a part in that. Said its director, Pierre Dieudonne, "If the next-generation Viper coupe comes along, then we can keep on building the success story. If we talk about the current car, it will still do well and please a lot of private teams, but it will be hard for them to fight against newer cars like Corvette. It will become difficult.

"There is a plan to have a coupe, but as far as we understand plans are on hold at the moment because of the [financial] situation at Chrysler. They need to introduce a coupe. An open car, a roadster, is mainly for leisure. If you want to build a race car, you want to start from a coupe."

The sound emitted from the 2003 Viper's side pipes will be modified by electronic mufflers. The sound-canceling mufflers impose less restriction on the flow of exhaust gas, so they let the engine make more power. And electronic mufflers can be switched off. For competition only, of course!

Agreed Roy Sjoberg, "If you are going to go racing, you want to go racing with a coupe, because of the aerodynamic benefits. Aerodynamics is as important as it is because of the top speeds you're running. If you are running 140 miles per hour, an open car is OK, If you are running 200 miles per hour an open car is not OK, unless you are going to do a full-out prototype.

"You are really back to the coupe configuration. Whether they see a need to do that, there is certainly a desire. The race guys, I'm sure, want to go racing. But whether there is the budget to do it, whether there is sufficient engineering impetus to do it and management impetus, at this time there would not be. Stay tuned."

"We as a company made a decision to get back into NASCAR," said Fernandez. "In this country, as much as I love road racing, NASCAR is where it's at. We wanted to do that as successfully as our other motorsports programs, so we needed to concentrate our efforts there. Even some of my guys are working on that program. So we said, 'We've won everything there is to win with the GTS-R, we want to focus our efforts on getting the VGX out there, we want to focus our effort on being successful with NASCAR.' And when we get down the line we'll take another good look at coming back and dominating the road racing circuits again."

We can be sure that the next racing Viper won't be met with the guffaws that greeted the company's first foray into road racing.

INDEX